MY BEST TO YOU

EACH MORNING

Rev. Donald C. Hancock

For Marlene
My Best to You ...
Don Hancock
March, 2012

DEDICATION

I lovingly dedicate this book of Devotional thoughts to my wife, Finetta, who has always been the wind beneath my wings, and to Bob Scaggs, the Director of my Sunday School Department, who gave me the privilege of bringing these devotionals to our Sunday School Department. I would also like to acknowledge the men and women of that Department, who listened to these devotionals initially and encouraged me to continue.

I am grateful to Patty Padgett, who encouraged me and guided me in many ways during this project. Lastly, I dedicate this and all of my writings to God who has given me all that I have.

TABLE OF CONTENTS

INTRODUCTION

Several years ago I retired as a Chaplain in a State School for the Developmentally Disabled, where I had ministered full time for 21 years. Before that I had been a Pastor for 14 years. So, after retirement I was delighted to be asked, about once a month, to prepare a ten minute devotional for my own Sunday School Department at First Baptist Church of Augusta, Georgia. The department is made up of Senior Adults, men and women, who accepted my offerings graciously.

Since each devotional was prepared prayerfully and with a great deal of thought and preparation, I thought that it might be helpful, on a broader scale, to other folks. So, I have prepared this little book, hoping that you, and perhaps some of your friends, might use it and find it beneficial for your own devotional use. That is my purpose in offering it to you.

Rev. Donald C. Hancock, Augusta, Georgia. January, 2012.

CHAPTER 1: FRIENDSHIP

Dianne Sawyer shared a story on ABC News that bears repeating. In the little town of Goodhue, Minn. it was much too early to think of Spring. There was certainly no green to be found anywhere. But something happened there that gives me a sense of "newness" and hope - you might even say awakening - that we usually feel with the beginning of Spring.

Howard Snitzer stopped in Goodhue to go to the grocery. Just before entering the store, Mr. Snitzer fell to the ground with a massive heart attack. Candace Cain, a shopper in the store, began to apply compressions to his chest. Someone called 911. Meanwhile, Roy and Al, from the repair shop across the street, rushed over and relieved Candace when her arms gave out. Roy and Al passed it on to a plumber, who gave it up to a carpenter, then to a county employee.

So it continued as two dozen pairs of hands kept Mr. Snitzer's heart pumping. When the medical helicopter arrived, 96 minutes later, there were twenty other people lined up. It seemed that, in Goodhue, a town so small it didn't even have a stop light, there was no shortage of people who care. No one even knew Mr. Snitzer. But they showed what friendship is all about.

There is something significant about the situation called "heart arrest". The victim might be the finest heart surgeon in the world, but he can't help himself at that moment. Yet a Boy Scout with a merit badge in First

Aid can save the surgeon's life. There is a bit of that same significance about the way that friendship works.

While few of us will experience heart arrest, all of us will experience "emotional arrest". Something will happen to us that will strike a blow to our emotional health and, because we are the person involved, we can not really help ourselves. Let me share a partial list of such happenings. Illness happens to yourself or someone close to you and your whole life is put on hold. You lose your driver's license because of vision problems, age, or physical injury. Your husband dies. Your pet dog, that you have shared life with for ten or fifteen years, goes to his reward. Divorce happens. These "happenings" are situations that, like heart arrest, you can not really handle yourself because you are the one it is happening to.

Now suppose such things are happening to people YOU know, which they are. Think of yourself for just a moment as the Boy Scout who happens to have gotten a merit badge on how to say, "I am so sorry!" While that might seem rather insignificant, it might be the very thing that will give a friend, an acquaintance, or even someone you hardly know, the help she needs at the moment. That is friendship even though it is just a few heart felt words.

CHAPTER 2: OUR SEEMING FAILURES

The month of March cradles St. Patrick's Day and I want to sing you an Irish song and tell you the story of its Irish author. Listen to this:

"Over there, over there, send the word, send the word over there,

That the Yanks are coming, the Yanks are coming, the drums rum tumming everywhere.

So prepare, say a prayer, send the word, send the word to beware,

We'll be over, we're coming over, and we won't be back 'til it's over over there!"

Now, the writer of this song was Irish to the core. He was as well known to those folks who lived before and during World War I as Bing Crosby, Frank Sinatra, and Rogers and Hammerstein were to our generation. His name was George M. Cohan.

Cohan sang, danced, and produced some of the top Broadway Musicals of his day. But the most important thing he did by far was to write "Over There". It became the song that gave America strength and courage during World War I. So important was that song to the American spirit that President Roosevelt presented Cohan with the Congressional Gold Medal, equivalent for civilians to the Medal of Honor for service men.

But when George M. Cohan died, early in World War II, he died with an unfulfilled personal ambition. He regretted that he had been unable to produce such a song as "Over There" for his country to have during that present war.

But he need not have worried, for just a few months after "Over There" was written, in the year 1918, such a song was already being formed in the mind of a young soldier who was in "boot" camp at Camp Upton in Yaphank, New York. The camp was preparing an all soldier variety show and the young soldier wrote a song for the show. For some reason it was rejected and the soldier, disappointed, put the song away in a box.

Twenty years later, in 1938, Kate Smith, a popular singer of the time, was planning a special Armistice Day radio show. She wanted a new song to be the highlight of her patriotic special, something that would give her country, facing probable war, a song to "hold on to". Ms. Smith went to Irving Berlin and explained her need and asked if he had anything she might use. He said something to the effect that "I have an old song I wrote way back in 1918 when I was a soldier in Yaphank, New York. I don't know if it is good enough but you are welcome to it". Kate Smith played it over and sang it and said, "Mr. Berlin, it is definitely good enough!" It was "God Bless America". It became the "Over There" of World War II.

I truly believe that God had kept that song safe and ready for those twenty years when it could easily have been thrown out, destroyed, and forgotten forever.

A similar thing happened to me in my career. I had gone to college and seminary to prepare for the chaplaincy. But when I graduated from seminary there were no chaplaincy positions open. I accepted a pastorate and served as a pastor for fourteen years. During that time I sent my resume to various chaplaincy opportunities but when several invitations came they were at times when I felt that I could not leave my church.

Finally, in 1970 a position opened and I was able to accept it. I was chaplain in that institution for 21 years and retired as Chief Chaplain. The unusual thing about that career change is that my resume had been sent, years before, to a fellow classmate from the seminary who was serving as a chaplain at the time. After keeping the resume for some time he sent it to another chaplain who kept it on file for over five years.

When that chaplain finally had an opening he went back into his old files and found my resume. Again, I believe that God had kept my resume safe and sound until it was time for my final success in becoming a chaplain. Though I had felt that my chaplaincy ambitions were unfulfilled, the time came when I would enjoy 21 years in that capacity.

I believe that God brings us into the world with certain goals that we are to accomplish. I believe that He files away certain experiences, lessons, and opportunities which appear in our lives at just the right time.

As we get a little nearer to the end of our lives, perhaps we have some regrets, things that we have done that we wish we had not, or, like George M. Cohan, things we wish we had done. Perhaps sometimes what we consider to be our failures are simply successes waiting to happen.

Irving Berlin thought his song had failed but it was just waiting for its time. Things that we might have said or done with the intention of helping someone might seem to have failed at first, but we have no way of knowing how much that word or action might influence the person when it is remembered later on.

Finally, there might be something that we really wanted to see happen, perhaps in our children. It might not even happen during our life time. Maybe it was not meant to happen in our life time. But we will still see it, when it happens, from our vantage point in Heaven.

Perhaps we should never label any of our endeavors as a failure. Who knows when God will bring something out of His old files and say, "Now the time is right for this to fly!"

CHAPTER 3: A FAMILY CHRISTMAS

It was a dark and snowy Christmas Eve in 1930, during the heart of the Great Depression. Mr. Sturgis was happy to be closing the Sturgis General Store after a very busy day. He looked forward to going home to his wife. His heart was warmed by the knowledge that he had supplied presents for most of the children in his little village – dollies, slingshots, balls and bats, even a few sleds and ice skates. Christmas shopping in those days was nothing like the extravagant buying sprees that we experience today, but most families managed to get some little item for each family member, especially for each child.

Just as he was about to turn off the lights and close the store, he heard a knock on the door. It was such a soft knock he almost did not hear it. He opened the door and there stood a small young woman, dressed in a ragged frock. Since it was already past closing time, Mr. Sturgis was tempted to say, "I am sorry but we are closed." But he looked into her face and somehow he could not turn her away. Besides, he often prayed that, if God had something special for him to do, He would give his heart a little "nudge". This seemed as though it might be one of those "nudges".

"I was just closing, Ma'am, but come on in. What can I do for you?"

"My name is Laura Adams, Mrs. Ned Adams. It is my little girl, Sir. My little Betty is seven years old and has never had a real Christmas. The girls at school had been talking about what they had asked Santy to bring them. I saw Betty crying and I asked her what was wrong. At first she said, 'Nothin' but when I kept after her she finally said, ' Well, Mama, Santy has never brought me anything and I know that you always say that, maybe next year, but I think that maybe Santy thinks I am too bad every year to get a present. I hear tell that bad little boys and girls don't get presents at Christmas time. But Mama, I honestly don't know of nothing real bad that I've done this year. I've really tried hard.'

"So, Mr. Sturgis, I can't bear to say, one more time, 'Maybe next year'. Now, it's just her and me since my Ned died and it is all I can do to keep us from going to the 'Poor Farm' to live. But if you've got a broken dolly that I could mend or a little game of 'jack stones' or just anything, Then I would come early or late and clean your store for as many days as you want me to pay for it. Would you consider doing that?"

Henry Sturgis looked her in the eyes and it was almost like looking at his own mother's sad eyes the year that his own daddy died. Henry was just a boy and he remembered how hard it had been for him and his mother. After a long pause, Henry said, "Mrs. Adams, here is what I would like for you to do. You see, my Sarah and I never had a child and we always missed having the joys of Christmas morning that other people talk about. So would you give us the pleasure of having you and Betty come to our house for Christmas dinner tomorrow? I would like for you to come at 9:00 o'clock to give us plenty of time for a real, sure enough, Santa Claus time at our Christmas tree. I want you to tell Betty that Santa Claus is going to bring her present to my house because I am one of his official helpers. Will you do that for me?"

"Oh, Mr. Sturgis, you don't know how happy that will make me and especially my Betty!"

After Mrs. Adams left, Henry Sturgis picked out his prettiest doll and several other things that a seven year old girl would like. Then he picked out some pretty yard goods that Mrs. Adams could use for a dress. He also picked a warm shawl that matched the material. He took some Christmas paper and ribbons with him so that he and Sarah could wrap up the presents.

The next morning he and Sarah welcomed Laura and Betty and they had a grand time opening presents and enjoying singing Christmas Carols. They had a wonderful Christmas dinner together and afterwards Mrs. Sturgis read the Christmas story. Then Henry said, "Laura and Betty, Sarah and I want to thank you for being part of our family today. You see, for years we prayed to God to give us children. But it never happened. We think that, maybe, He has finally answered our prayers by sending you to us! Maybe you can be like a daughter and grand daughter to us and we can be like parents and grand parents to you!"

Betty and Laura thought that was a grand idea, and that Christmas day began a long tradition of regular "family gatherings" that lasted until Ma and Pa Sturgis went to be with God. Betty and Laura thanked God every night for giving them their new family.

CHAPTER 4: A MEMORIAL DAY FISH STORY

I call this a Memorial Day Fish Story but actually it is a good story for any day! You might say that it is a "fantasy", not because fish do not talk – they certainly communicate among themselves or they could not function as they do. It might be called a fantasy because we are not usually able to hear and understand them as we will today.

I conceived the idea for this story several Sundays ago when my Pastor preached a sermon about what happened one day when Jesus' disciples were fishing. In the Gospel of John, chapter 21, we read how, after the resurrection of Jesus, Peter decided to go fishing. Several other disciples went with him. They fished all night but caught nothing. The next morning Jesus was standing on the shore and he called to them, "have you caught anything?" The disciples did not know that it was Jesus but called back to him, "No, nothing at all!" Jesus then said, "cast on the other side of the boat." They did as he said and caught so many fish immediately that their net would not hold all of them. Jesus then invited them to bring their fish and then eat a breakfast that he had been preparing. This story became one of the important teaching miracles of Christ.

My part of the story comes from the following scenario. Several years and many fish generations after the Jesus story above took place, a grandmother fish is talking to her grand children fish on "Fish Memorial Day". And, yes, of course fish observe Memorial Day! In this scene

they are in Lake Galilee. The conversation goes
something like this.

"Now, children, I want you to remember that today is
"Fish Memorial Day". It is a day set aside to remember
our loved ones who have passed away. I want to tell you
the story of one of our ancestors . Abraham Bass was
your great, great, great grandfather. He lived here in the
great Galilee Lake back when Jesus lived among us."

"Well, there came a day when Jesus' disciples were in
their boat, fishing. On this particular day, God wanted to
perform a miracle to inspire the disciples. So God talked
to all of the fish in the whole lake and told them that He
wanted them to do him a special favor. He wanted them
to all go to the other side of the lake and stay there the
whole night so the disciples would not catch anything at
all. Now, your grandfather Abraham was there and also
his cousin, Abigail, who passed this story on to us.

"So, all of the fish stayed on the other side of the lake all
night. They enjoyed playing a joke on the disciples.
Then God said something that sent a shiver up the spines
of all of the fish that were there that day. He said that He
needed volunteers who would give up their lives in order
to teach a very special lesson to Jesus' disciples. A large
number of the fish backed away, but God had many
volunteers who were willing to give their lives that day.
And your great grandfather, Abraham Bass was one of
those volunteers."

"Can I ask a question?" said little Timothy Bass. "Of course", said the grandmother. "Did God know who grandfather Abraham was? Did He know his name?" "Yes, Timothy", said the grandmother.   "He knows your name and my name. In fact, humans have a saying that 'God even knows the number of hairs on every person's head'. We fish have a similar saying that 'God knows how many scales are on our backs'. Humans say that God takes notice when even a sparrow falls. We fish like to believe that God knows when even a little minnow dies."

"So, your great grandfather Abraham gladly volunteered to God, and at a certain time they all swam into the disciples' nets and were hauled into the boat. For these many years people have read about what Peter and James and John and Nathaniel and others did on that day. But they never heard about how Abraham Bass gave his life so that Jesus could teach a very important lesson to his disciples. But we all know what grandfather Abraham did. And God knows too. You see, children, sometimes we think that our leaders and our teachers are the only ones who do things that are important. But I want you to know that, when any one of us does anything at all for each other, God notices it and it is every bit as important in His sight as what great grandfather Abraham did for Jesus those many years ago."

And now I say to each of you who is hearing my story right now. Yes, the Ministers in our church do very important and helpful things every day. But when each of us, no matter how old we are, gives a word of encouragement or gives a smile, or a pat on the back to one another, it is just as much doing work for God as it would be if we were someone like Billy Graham or even Jesus Himself. In fact Jesus would probably say that when one of us does something to help someone else, it is just like we were doing it for Jesus himself.

On this Memorial Day we honor those that have given their lives in service to others. But let us not forget that we each are giving our lives in service to God and others each time we do a random act of kindness.

CHAPTER 5: WHEN IT RAINS ON YOUR PARADE

April is a time when we expect some additional rain to fall, and it is sometimes an inconvenience.

Barbara Streisand sings a song called "Don't Rain On My Parade". The idea is that she has her life all lined up the way she wants it and she doesn't want anybody or anything to cloud up and rain on her plans.

All of us have our own parade and there are a lot of things that can cause rain, like financial problems, career problems and, especially, health problems. Our dentist, who served us well for over thirty years before he retired, used to look into my mouth at the teeth he had filled, replaced, and propped up, and he would say, "your mouth is an accident waiting to happen". I suppose that many of our doctors look at our bodies, especially those of us older folks, and say the same thing - "This is an accident waiting to happen!" There are many things that can rain on our parade at any particular moment.

But Al Jolson, a singer in the 30's and 40's, had a song that took a very positive approach to such rain. It went like this:

"Life is not a highway strewn with flowers, Still it holds a goodly share of bliss. When the sun gives way to April Showers, Here's a thought that we should never miss.

Though April showers may come your way, They bring the flowers that bloom in May;

And if it's raining, have no regrets, Because it isn't raining rain you know, It's raining violets.

And when you see clouds upon the hill, you soon will see crowds of daffodils;

So keep on looking for the bluebird, and listening for his song,
Whenever April showers come along". *

The Apostle Paul, in the New Testament, expressed a similar thought when he said, and this is a paraphrase, "Troubles bring about patience in your life. And patience leads us to have experience with God. And our experience with God leads us to have hope and confidence in God". *

Al Jolson was pointing out that, even though we enjoy the sunshine, if there was no occasional rain our lives would miss the blessing of having the beautiful flowers. Paul is giving the same thought a spiritual application by saying that, even though we enjoy the times when our lives move along smoothly, we need to recognize that the difficulties we experience in life force us to grow and become our best selves, and they force us also to get to know God better than we would otherwise.

In a way, Paul was just rewording Mr. Jolson's song to say something like this:

"Though trouble's showers may come along, They bring the patience that makes you strong;

And if there's worry, God will calm your fears,

Because He's always there to hold your hand and dry away your tears.

And when you see clouds that block your view, You soon will see God come shining through,

So keep on looking for God's blessing and listening for His song,

Whenever some new trouble comes along".

When I was a small boy I would sometimes come in with a scraped knee and my mother would always run for the little bottle of iodine. I would immediately begin to cry and say, "That will burn, Mama, that will burn!" She would always say, "Well, that burning lets us know that the iodine is killing all those bad germs!"

Paul would say that, when we feel the hurt of trouble, that hurting lets us know that the trouble is doing its job of making us stronger and more patient and is drawing us closer to our God. Paul would probably add, "So we will glory in our troubles, knowing that troubles bring about patience and patience brings about experience and hope because the love of God is felt in our hearts".

So, when illness comes or we hear of some problem that our loved ones are having, or even when we suffer the loss of someone very close to us or come face to face with our own last days, let us know that such trouble, while very painful, is temporary, and can lead to a greater sense of the Presence of God, if we will allow it to happen.

*April Showers. Music by Louis Silvers, Lyrics by B.G. De Sylva.

* Romans 5: verses 3 and 4. (Paraphrased)

CHAPTER 6: VALENTINE'S DAY

We are approaching Valentine's Day and, as I think about that day I think about some imaginary Valentines that might have been sent.

FROM A YOUNG MAN TO HIS GIRL FRIEND

Dearest Valentine:

I love you so much that:

I would climb the highest mountain to reach you,

I would swim the deepest ocean to see your face,

I would cross the widest desert to be where you are!

And I will be there to see you Saturday if it doesn't rain.

SOME VALENTINES THAT MIGHT HAVE BEEN SENT FROM THE BIBLE

FROM JACOB TO RACHEL

Dear Rachel. Be my Valentine:

If you will be my Valentine,

I will work seven years taking care of sheep

With no pay, just so I can marry you!

And if your father happens to trick me,

Which I think he is quite capable of doing,

Then I will work another seven years

Just so I can marry you.

Now, if that isn't love I don't know what is!

From Your Jacob

FROM JOSEPH TO MARY

Dearest Mary,

I know that some of the neighbors are

Raising questions about the little one

That we are expecting.

But I wanted you to know that I trust you

And I know that you have always been

Faithful to me.

I also believe God's Angel and his

Promise that we are in the will of God.

I am looking forward to our walking together

In the path that God has set for us.

Your loving espoused husband, Joseph.

FROM GOD TO HIS CHILDREN

My Dear Children,

I made the world and trees and grass,

The skies and all the seas.

The monkeys, fish, and elephants

And even bumble bees.

And then I made you, man and wife,

And liked what I had done.

Then I realized I more than liked you,

I loved you! Every one!

Love, God

AND THIS IS THE VALENTINE THAT I WOULD
LIKE TO THINK MIGHT COME FROM US TO GOD

Dear God,

Your love for me makes me want to

Love you more!

Please help me to be full of love for You,

As you deserve!

And please help me to be your Valentine

To all the people that you let me be with

In this world: My family, My friends,

And everybody else!

Love, Your Child

Prayer: We DO love you, God. Help us to love you more!

CHAPTER 7: SHOWING LOVE TO OTHERS

In 1939 I lived in Port St. Joe, Florida. I was in the first grade and I had never been to a movie theater, because there was none in our town. But one was built that year and we could hardly wait until it was completed. On the billboard it said, "Coming The Wizard of Oz!".

What a wonderful movie that was! It was one of the first movies to use the new technicolor process. It was not color through the whole movie, just the second part. The first part of the movie was in black and white.

The main characters, other than Dorothy, played two parts. The Tin Man, Scarecrow, and Lion were actually friends of the family in the black and white segment. Frank Morgan, who played the Wizard, also played a traveling side show pitch man named Professor Marvel in the black and white segment.

Professor Marvel had to have a particular kind of coat. It had to be a sort of genteel garment but it had to have the appearance of being old and shabby. The wardrobe department of the studio went into downtown L.A. and procured a rack full of coats and brought them back to the studio. Frank Morgan and the Movie Director went through all of the coats, about fifty of them, and found one that looked just right. It was a "Prince Albert" coat with velvet lapels. And it was old and shabby. It fit Frank Morgan perfectly.

They were filming the black and white segment in the summer time and they did not have air conditioned sound stages then. So, under the lights it became very hot and Mr. Morgan perspired profusely. During a break he opened the coat to fan himself and pulled out the pockets so they could dry. He casually looked down and saw the name of the tailor who had made the coat and, presumably the name of the owner written in indelible ink.

When Frank Morgan saw the name he was astonished and immediately wired the tailor in Boston to confirm the name. When the film was finished, Mr. Morgan personally presented the coat to the owner's widow. The coat had belonged to the gentleman who had written the book from which "The Wizard of Oz" had been filmed, Mr. Frank Baum. Mrs. Baum had long forgotten that old coat but I am sure that it would become a very treasured reminder of her husband.

This fascinating story reminds me of a story in the Bible, in the book of Acts. It is the story of a lady by the name of Dorcas. She became ill and died. The apostle Peter was called to her home and found a large group of widow ladies there. They had brought coats and other garments that Dorcas had made for them as random acts of kindness.

As I reread that story I thought, and please forgive me for such a fanciful idea – I thought that, perhaps, when we all get to Heaven we will find that one of God's favorite activities might be for Him to drag out a long coat rack full of coats. Each coat will represent a random act of kindness that we have long forgotten.

As He reads out the name on each coat He will tell of this or that person that we helped with a smile or encouragement or some other needed support. He will remind us that Christ said when we do these random acts of kindness for others it is the same as if we are doing it for Him.

I truly believe that our main purpose for coming to the earth is not to amass wealth or power, but to help each other as we meet the different challenges that our lives present.

My Best To You Each Morning

CHAPTER 8: GOD STILL WORKS IN OUR LIVES TODAY

In Acts, Chapter 9 we have the story of the Apostle Paul's Damascus Road Experience. Paul (Or Saul, as he was called then) had an experience with God and God said for him to go to Damascus and wait. Then he told a man named Ananias to go to the street called Straight and to the home of a man named Judas. He was to inquire about a man named Saul. In the mean time God told Saul that he would have a visit from a man named Ananias. Out of this meeting came great blessings. God was working in all of that!

In the very next chapter of Acts is another story of God working. God told a centurion named Cornelius to send his men to Joppa and inquire of a man named Simon Peter. In the mean time God gave Peter a teaching vision in which a sheet came down from Heaven with all kinds of animals that were considered unclean by the Jews. God said, "Kill and eat". Peter said, "No, God, I can't eat anything that is unclean". God said, "Don't judge anything that I have made as unclean". While Peter was wondering what that could mean, Cornelius' men came in and asked Peter to go see Cornelius, an unclean Gentile. Then Peter realized what the dream was about. Out of this came the great teaching about allowing the Gentiles to become Christians. God was working!

Sure, that happened in Bible times, but I think those things happen very often in our lives today. When I was in high school I was trying to decide if God was really calling me to preach. One afternoon I was home by myself. I was so desperate to know God's will that I was kneeling in the living room by the sofa and pleading for an answer. I was not used to kneeling when I prayed, so I really was desperate. While I was kneeling the door bell rang. A man that I had never seen before said, I am the pastor of the Assembly of God church down the street and I just wanted to give you this. He handed me a little tract that said, as well as I can remember, something like, "God Is Calling You". God was working.

Now, that was a long time ago but just listen to what happened last week. On Monday I made my monthly visit to a Nursing home and we always sing the Old Songs especially the World War II songs, you know, Mairzy Doats, Three Little Fishes, Don't Sit Under the Apple Tree, etc. One song I never learned was Rosie the Riveter. A lady asked me about that song a month ago and I told her I would learn it. But I forgot. Well, last Monday she asked me about it and I had to tell her that I had forgotten but I tore off a piece of paper and wrote Rosie the Riveter on it and put it in my pocket.

That was Monday. I kept the piece of paper but was forgetting to go to the computer and learn the song. Well, in the Sunday morning newspaper there was a two page article about Rosie and about a lady who had been a Riveter in World War II and has formed a "Rosie the Riveter" club with 3000 members. I emailed the lady and told her that my mother was a Riveter in a ship yard in Savannah, Georgia in 1943. I also went to the computer and printed off the words to Rosie the Riveter. God had gotten my attention, and God is working.

On Tuesday, I went to a Senior luncheon at a neighborhood church. I have been needing a new hearing aid and was not sure where to go. The speaker at the luncheon was an audiologist . I happened to sit next to her during our eating time. It turned out that I knew her father and brother from my work as a chaplain. My wife knew her brother in law and nephew from her work as a school teacher. I think I know where to go for my next hearing aid, and I think God was working.

On Wednesday of the same week We had a Chinese lady at our home. Beth* is a Licensed Practical Nurse who is studying to pass her State Board Examination to be a Registered Nurse. She has taken the test once and did not pass. We wanted to help her study the areas in which she was weak on the test, but we were really feeling inadequate for the job. We normally teach her English but we are not fluent with the medical concepts. Suddenly I thought of a nurse that I know through my hospice work. Cathy* has recently retired from active nursing. I called her and she came right over. She just lives around the block from me. I introduced her to Beth and she told Beth that her daughter had recently gone to China and had adopted her daughter from ...and she named the city. "That's the city where I was born", said Beth. Beth and Cathy hit it off immediately and have made a time to study together. Again, God was working.

On Sunday morning I went to my regular Men's Sunday school class. I explained that I had missed last Sunday because my son, who is studying to be a Methodist Minister and has a small pastorate in a nearby town, was celebrating his first anniversary with the church. One of the 12 members of my Sunday School class came up to me after class and said, "I grew up in that town and my sister goes to that church". The brother in my class of twelve and his sister in my son's congregation that averages about 30 in the congregation on a good day. Small world! And God is still working in my world.

* Names have been changed to protect privacy.

CHAPTER 9: THE DAY I SHOOK HANDS WITH SENATOR TED KENNEDY

On Monday of this week I was in my basement, cleaning out old "stuff". Out of a box fell three old photographs. I picked them up. One was a picture of Senator Ted Kennedy. The other two told the story of how I had the picture of "Teddy".

About 30 years ago I was a chaplain at a state facility for the retarded (as they were labeled in those days). Jimmy Carter was president and Washington was the center of activity for the improvement of quality of life for those who were disabled in any capacity. So I and several other staff members took a group of our clients to visit Washington and appear at the conference for the disabled.

It was a wonderful experience and several of our clients were able to appear on the program. But the main part for all of us was to visit the Capitol and see the Senate "in action." We met our Senator, Sam Nunn, from Georgia and he posed for a picture with the group. We saw several Senators just walking in the halls and they stopped to greet us. But the highlight of the day was when we saw Senator Kennedy out in front of the Capitol building and all of us got to shake his hand. I took a close up picture of this man who, even then, was a main pillar of our national political life. He looked so young and approachable. His dark hair and smiling "Irish" face beaming. I got that on my camera.

When I got home I showed that picture to all of my friends and family. But then, instead of having an album of "my trip to Washington", the pictures got shunted into a box of "old stuff".

Then on Monday, August 24, over 30 years later, God and/or His Angels (or was it just coincidence? You decide) let that picture and two group pictures fall out on the floor. I saw the other two pictures and noticed who the other two staff members were. That night I sent the two group pictures and the picture of Senator Kennedy to one of the other two staff members, but did not have the email of the second, so on Tuesday evening I called the lady to get her e mail address.

The next morning she called me. She said, "did you know that Senator Kennedy died near the time that you called me last night to send me his picture?" I think she felt that this was more than coincidence. I tend to agree with her. When I sent the picture it did not even occur to me that he was near death, for I had not watched the news that day. It is as if the whole situation had happened so that I might have a little part in honoring the Senator in the last few hours of his life and then also today as I write my few words about the day I "shook Senator Kennedy's hand". Whatever your politics might be, I felt that it was an honor the day that I met him. I believe that when seeming coincidences happen like this, it is at least possible that God had a hand in it. God does seem to work in a mysterious way sometimes.

CHAPTER 10: SPARKLING GEMS THAT WERE "ALMOST NOT DISCOVERED"

There are stories that I have heard all of my adult life about people and things that were almost overlooked or rejected, only to become a shining success later on. I wondered if these stories were true or just "good stories". So I did a bit of research and found out that these stories that follow are, indeed, true. Now I want to share them with you!

The first story is of a young man who loved music and decided to study the cello, his instrument of choice. In 1886, he got a job playing cello with an opera company that was going to tour South America. When the troupe played the opera, "Aida", in Rio de Janeiro, the audience was so disappointed with the performance of the conductor, that they booed him off the stage. Someone in the orchestra, who had been impressed with the musical ability of the young cello player, asked if he would try to finish the performance of the opera. Even though he had not had any experience conducting in public, he walked to the platform and finished conducting the opera totally from memory, to the great joy and delight of the audience.

So magnificent was this first performance, that , even though he returned brieflly to playing the cello, his notoriety raised him to world fame as a conductor. After traveling all over the world for a number of years, he settled in America. The National Broadcasting Company created a symphony orchestra just for him and he was their conductor from 1937 until his health failed in 1954. This young cello player could easily have been overlooked except for his being called on to "save the day" for his fellow musicians. This young man's name was Arturo Toscanini, perhaps the greatest and best known conductor of the Twentieth Century. 1

Another young man, who was almost overlooked, was a young dancer. He had done some dancing on stage, but really wanted to get into the fairly new medium of the movies. Finally, in the early days of the Great Depression, he was able to get his "foot in the door" by being accepted for a screen test. There is some discrepancy about the actual wording of the screen test report but it was something like this: " He can't sing, he can't act, he is getting bald, he can dance a little". In his first film he had a short dancing part. In his second film, "Flying Down to Rio" his name was fifth down the list, but he did get to dance with one of the main stars. Then, after that, he made ten more films with that same star, Ginger Rogers. He was an Academy Award winner, was hailed as the fifth greatest male star of all time by the American Film Institute, and played in 31 musical films. His career spanned 76 years. A pretty good record for a fellow who "can't sing, can't act, is balding," and "can dance a little". This gem that was almost overlooked was Fred Astaire. 2.

Now, let us turn to another gem, only this time it is not a person but a movie. I saw this movie on television last week. I had heard of its uniqueness for years but had never seen it. This movie was sort of a "red headed step child" at MGM when it was created in the early 1950's. It was in competition with another movie, "Brigadoon", which was in production at the same time. MGM even siphoned money from this little underprivileged movie to build up its favored child. Yet, in spite of its overlooked status, it garnered a 1954 Oscar nomination for Best Picture, was counted among the Top Ten Musicals in a book , "Top Ten of Film", by Russel Ash, and in 2006 it ranked # 21 on the American Institute's list of the best musicals of all time. I would recommend that you see this one if you ever have the chance. This little gem that, perhaps, almost didn't get made, was "Seven Brides for Seven Brothers". 3.

Another diamond that almost didn't get a chance to sparkle was a song. It was brought to life by Frank Sinatra, who, apparently despised it from the beginning. In fact he was quoted as saying that it was " a piece of (excrement)" and that it was "the worst (bleep) song I ever heard". Yet he decided to record it anyway and it won him a Grammy for the Best Male Pop Vocal Performance. The song itself won a Grammy for the Best Record of the year in 1966, and the album was one of the most commercially successful albums of all times. You might remember Frank humming "dooby dooby doo" at the end, as though he were "tossing it away". It was, "Strangers In the Night"!.4.

My last little shining gem that almost "got tossed" is also a song. It first saw the light of day through a recording of a famous cowboy movie and recording star, Gene Autry. Gene did not feel, at first, that the song was worth considering. He felt that it was just too silly to be dignified with a record. But, it is reported (and I could not verify this) that when he went home and told his wife about this silly thing that he had been asked to record, she said something like, "Oh, why not try it. It couldn't hurt!" As a result, Gene reluctantly tagged it on at the tail end of a recording session and did it with just one take. But this little jewel would not stay hidden. For, after it was recorded in 1949, it sold 2 million single copies that year alone. It has become one of the best selling songs of all time, second only to Bing Crosby's "White Christmas". Even now it steals the airwaves every Christmas as it "helps to light Santa's sleigh". It is, of course, "Rudolph, the Red Nosed Reindeer"! 5.

Now, the moral of this story, if indeed it needs a moral, is this: If you think that you have a talent that has not yet been recognized or if you feel that you are undervalued by your peers, just keep on being yourself and perhaps you, like those gems mentioned above, will get your opportunity to shine!

1.http://en.wikipedia.org/wiki/Arturo_Toscanini

2.http://en.wikipedia.org/wiki/Fred_Astaire#1933-1939:_Astaire_and_Rogers_at_RKO

3.http://en.wikipedia.org/wiki/Seven_Brides_for_Seven_Brothers_(film

4.http://en.wikipedia.org/wiki/Strangers_in_the_Night

5 .http://www.cmt.com/artists/az/autry_gene/bio.jhtml

Chapter 11: THE PERSPECTIVE SWITCH

A young couple had a seven year old son that they were worried about. He was a perpetual optimist and they were afraid his optimism would allow everyone to "walk all over him" when he got out into the "real world". So at Christmas time, when he wrote a letter to Santa asking for a pony, they noted that all he could talk about was that pony that Santa was absolutely, definitely going to bring him. They decided that, to give him a strong and healthy dose of disappointment they would get some horse manure from a farmer friend, box it up and wrap it for Christmas. Surely this would teach him once and for all not to expect to get everything he asked for.

So Christmas came with the little boy racing downstairs to ride his pony. As they opened the presents he opened the box of manure with increasing glee and when he peered into the box he said, "I told you, I told you Santa would bring me a pony!"

"But son, that is just a box of manure, not a pony!"

"But Dad, that means the pony is around here someplace! Let's find it!" We'll come back to the pony story a little later.

Several nights ago there was a full moon on a very clear night and it was directly over head. You could almost read a newspaper outside. But have you ever been out in the country where there were no street lights on a night when there was no moon at all? You can't see your hand in front of you. But the problem is not the darkness but in our sight. On that same dark night when we can't see anything an owl in the top of a tree can see a little mouse running on the ground. So, wouldn't it be nice if God had given us a switch so that on those dark nights we could switch to "night vision". Well, God did not give us a night vision switch but he did give us something even more important and more valuable. A Perspective Switch.. A Perspective switch can not change how your eyes see at night but it can change the way that you look at the events in your life.

There is a story in the Bible that tells how God gave Adam the privilege of naming every animal. Whatever he called it that was how it would be called .That was quite an honor. But the gift and the privilege he gave to us is the privilege of naming everything that happens to us. Everything that happens in our lives remains nameless until we call it either a blessing or a curse. Even if it is something that everyone else would typically call a tragedy, like sickness, an accident, financial disaster, God gives us the sole right to name it.Whatever we name it determines what it becomes in our lives

The little boy in the pony story was using his perspective switch. While he did not get the pony that Christmas, he had a much better chance of getting a pony later on by continuing to look for it than if he had run up to his bed in utter devastation and anger.

Now, I am not talking about some sort of neurotic Pollyanna approach to life in which we call something that is black white in hopes that it might magically change. No, I am talking about actually altering the meaning and effects of what would ordinarily be a devastating event by simply switching our perspective.

In a book that I am currently reading, a young father gets influenza in the early 20th century and dies after a few days of illness, leaving a wife and young children. This was enough to ruin the lives of this family. But with his dying breath, as his wife cried sadly, he changed the perspective of everyone by saying, "Hush, Dear, God is in it! That phrase stayed with the wife and children. It changed their perspective to the extent that even the grand children of this dying man often quoted those words when trouble came. "Hush, God is in it."

We should not call otherwise horrible things a blessing just because it is a nice thing to do or because we can fool ourselves into believing a lie. We should call these things a blessing because millions of people have found out that it works. By naming these happenings blessings it opens the door to allow them to become just that, a blessing.

I have heard people with just about any bad happening that you can name, say, "it is the best thing that ever happened to me". They will say things like, "When I got Aids I was devastated, but it is the best thing that ever happened to me because I found out what life is all about". "I have cancer but it has become a wonderful blessing because I have developed a compassion and a sensitivity that I never had before". "I thank God that He has used that wreck I was in to show me the wrong direction of my life." On and on, people finding blessing because they were able to switch their perspective and name a devastating event a blessing instead of a curse. Yes, we also have the privilege of naming it a curse if we want to. It will just as surely become that, a curse!

Nor does it have to be such a really bad event. All day long you and I are privileged to name all the little things that happen either a blessing or a curse, a loss or a lesson, a problem or an opportunity. But we decide. No one else is given that privilege!

It does not mean that we can not be a little aggravated that little inconveniences happen or sorry that so called "awful" things happen. It is only human to feel aggravated and sad and sorry and even fearful. But it does mean that, after going through some of these human emotions, we can switch our perspective and say, "Well, there is blessing to be found in this and it will be easier for me to find it if I look for it. So, yes, I am going to label this "a Blessing!"

CHAPTER 12: THE LOVE OF GOD

Last night I dreamed that I received a telephone call from a radio station and the announcer was wondering where I was. I had promised to be there to deliver a sermon on his radio program and was I going to be there. I remembered that I had promised and had forgotten all about it. I assured him that "I was on my way!" I had not prepared for this and on the way to the station I realized that I had not even brought my Bible. I remembered a sermon that I had preached years before and literally spent the rest of my dream remembering the details of that sermon. Then I woke up at 4:00 A.M, came to the computer, and here I am. This is the way the sermon bubbled up from my heart and soul, even without benefit of my Bible. I promise that this is a shorter version than the one in my dream!

WHAT DOES GOD WANT MOST?

If you were to ask me my favorite passage from the Bible I would have to give you two of them. The first - "God was in Christ, reconciling the world unto Himself, and he has given unto us the ministry of reconciliation." Have you ever had a real break in fellowship with someone you loved? Perhaps, this break lasted a long time, maybe even years? Then one day with many tears and much hugging you "made up"? You remember how delicious that was? That is what reconciliation is in this verse. God, in His love, is always about bringing us to Himself in this sort of "tears and hugs reunion".

The second favorite verse comes from a story in the Old Testament. Young David, before he was King, had a small army of men and they lived for a number of days in a field that they shared with some shepherds who were keeping sheep owned by a certain well- to- do gentleman farmer. His men protected the sheep and shepherds from wild animals on several occasions. At one point the men were very hungry and so David sent one of his men to the owner with a request for a little food, a few scraps of bread, from his generosity. The not-so-wise or generous gentleman said something like, "why should I give him bread, I don't owe him anything?" One of the shepherds present recounted how David's men on several occasions had saved the sheep from wild animals. But the man was unmoved and kept to his refusal.

As David prepared to detach this man from his life, the man's wife heard of the situation and brought David a generous amount of food along with her request for David to spare her husband. She said something to the effect that, "Yes, he is stupid and, yes, he is a miser, but he's the only husband I've got. Please, please, for my sake spare him."

David took pity on this lady, Abigail, and spared the man's life. Here is where my favorite Old Testament verse comes in. Abigail says, "May the soul of my lord, David, be brought together in the Bundle of Life with God forever". (That is the way I remember it without benefit of Bible before me!)

During the great depression of the 30's there were many men who "rode the rails" in freight trains looking for jobs. They were called hobo's. Many of them were homeless and would tie all of their few earthly possessions - their precious few things - in a little bundle in something like a bandanna and tie it on the end of a stick. This is the picture that I get from Abigail's blessing. God and David being tied up together forever in a little bundle of "God's precious things".

So, my favorite two verses in the whole Bible speak to me of His love. First, His main purpose in life is to bring us back into fellowship with Him (a broken fellowship which He never wanted in the first place) . He has asked us to help Him do that same reconciling with all of His creation on earth. Second, that God wants all of us to enjoy being bound up in the closest kind of fellowship with each other and with Himself, forever and ever and ever!

That was the sermon that bubbled up from my heart in my dream last night. I woke up before I got to preach it on the radio. So I just got to share it with you. I hope you didn't mind.

My Best To You Each Morning

CHAPTER 13:: EMBARRASSING MEMORIES OF A MINISTER

The Pastor of a church has many embarrassing moments that are painful at the moment but bring a smile when we look back on them years later. I would like to share a few of these from my own "basket of goodies".

My first church was what we called a "seminary church". That is, I was there on the week-ends while I attended seminary. My wife was the church Pianist. During my time there I had my first wedding and my first funeral.

THE WEDDING

The church did not have a suitable space for the wedding party to dress. This was a village church and there were houses just across the road from the church. The bride and groom dressed at one of those homes and apparently were in a very happy mood in preparation for the nervous event that they faced.. As I looked out of the front door of the church, I saw the wedding party "processing" across the road.

They had broad smiles on their faces and I would describe their whole demeanor as "very laid back". I really wondered if there could be a serious moment in this service. To make a long story shorter, when I asked the bride, "Do you take this man to be your lawfully wedded husband, the bride smiled broadly ...and smiled...and smiled. But no words came from her mouth. I whispered, "say 'I do' ". She finally got those words out, surrounded by giggles. The rest of the service was likewise charged with jovial suspense.

THE FUNERAL
My first funeral was also in this church. It was the funeral of an infant. Unlike the other stories in my recollections, it was not funny in recall, but it deserves to be included since it certainly was a time of embarrassment. It was summer time and all of the windows of the church were open. I had spent a great deal of time trying to find just the right words for such a sad occasion.

I was leaning heavily on the notes that I had carefully prepared. When the time for the sermon arrived, I opened my Bible and the notes quickly blew away with the breeze from the windows. Not only did they blow off of my Bible to the floor, it was not the floor that I was standing on but the lower floor where the casket was placed. There was no way to retrieve those three pages of notes. I did the best that I could but after the service I had no idea at all of what I had said.

THE UNUSUAL CHAIR
Being a city boy there was a lot that I had to learn in a country church. In one of my first pastoral visits, I went to the home of an elderly lady who was bed ridden. Her son lived with her. After visiting the mother at her bedside I was sitting with the son, trying to make sensible small talk. I looked around the room in order to make some complimentary comment. "That is a very unusual chair," I said, spotting a chair with a box - like

bottom.

"You do know what that is?" said he. "I guess not", said I. "That is a commode chair". "Oh", said I.

THE BAPTISM

In my second pastorate there was a baptismal pool just in back of the pulpit, with curtains that could be opened when someone was to be baptized. In a Baptist church this was done by fully immersing the person underwater. I had very carefully rehearsed for my first baptismal service. I had what I was going to say well planned. I had talked the lady that I was going to baptize through the procedure. There was a welded bracket on the bottom of the pool under which the feet should be placed in order to anchor them.

All was ready. I stepped into the pool with my wading boots. I helped the lady down the steps into the pool as the church members watched. This lady weighed about 200 pounds and was about five feet tall, very buoyant. When she got to the proper place in front of me, she seemed to be doing a new type of shuffle dance. She could not find the bracket. But she stopped shuffling so I felt that all was well.

I said the proper pronouncement, ending with, "in the name of the Father and of the Son and of the Holy Spirit." Then I proceeded to push her back under the water. I pushed and pushed. He feet rose up. Her legs rose up. Her whole torso rose up. If her entrance into Heaven were totally dependent on her being fully immersed (which of course it isn't) then I would be duly concerned about her qualifications.

THE EXPLOSION

On another occasion there was a baptism planned for the morning service. Usually this was done during an evening service. That allowed all afternoon for the baptismal pool to be filled. But for a morning service I had turned on the water during Sunday School and allowed it to continue running during the sermon. A deacon was monitoring the water level while I preached.

One interesting thing about the baptismal pool was that it was fabricated of sheet steel and the bottom curved up in a little convex arc. Therefore, when the water reached a certain weight, the convex bottom would shift to concave with a very loud "bang". I did not know this! Just as I got to a very important point in my sermon the "explosion" occurred just three feet in back of me. I turned and yelled with full voice, "Oh, God!"
The congregation howled!

THE FUNERAL PROCESSION

In Kentucky, the practice was for the Pastor's car to lead the funeral procession to the cemetery. I was fully briefed on the route to take and was fairly confident until the undertaker said, "you can't miss it". That statement always worries me.

Well, after the service in the church I went out to my car, which was prepared for me in the front of the line. I led the procession of about 30 vehicles down the route prescribed until I made a wrong turn. A sheriff's car overtook me. I rolled down my window. "You are going away from the cemetery," he said. "Why don't I follow you?" I said. "You WILL follow me!" he said.

THE SERVICE AT THE GRAVE
The service at the graveside is usually very brief. I had asked the Funeral Director about the procedure and he said when I finished my message to give him a nod and he would take over from there. He did not know that the seminary does not offer "Funerals 101 and that the only funeral I had attended in my memory was that of my grandmother when I was four years old.

When I was "finished", I nodded to the Director. He did nothing. I did nothing. After a very awkward pause he walked over and whispered in my ear, "Pass by the family". I very quietly and reverently walked by the family and stood by the Director. He leaned over and whispered in my ear, "I meant to say some words of condolence to the family."
I said, "Oh".

So, even though our Pastor is far beyond such ministerial mistakes, let's remember him in our prayers. He is still facing difficult decisions every day. Some of them are not humorous like these that I have mentioned. He needs our support every day.

My Best To You Each Morning

CHAPTER 14: BLESS YOU

I was in a home improvement store last night, ordering a new kitchen counter top. While the salesman was writing up the order I sneezed. The salesman immediately said, "bless you". I thanked him and truly appreciated the gesture. I always do. I had the impression that, if I sneezed again he would have repeated the blessing. I did not "grow up" with that as a family custom, and I sometimes wonder what the motivation might be.

Originally, I understand, it was a superstition that, during a sneeze, the soul is very close to leaving the body for good. The "bless you" was an attempt to keep that from happening. In modern times I suspect that it is sometimes a force of habit and perhaps even an act of respect for the mother or father who taught the person to do that. But I think that it is often a gesture of genuine good will toward the person.

Perhaps it would be a really good habit to get into. No, not the repeating of a phrase like, "Bless you", necessarily, but a genuine directing of our total personality in some form of good will gesture toward others on occasions of meeting or at times when we have reason to believe that the person needs extra help, a "Bless You" in, perhaps, some other form.

Some oriental countries show respect, upon meeting someone, with a slight bowing of the head - the greater the respect, the lower the head. I wish that we had such a gesture as that in America. The nearest that most of us come to that is a smile and a hello.

There has been an attempt lately to establish a gesture especially for the purpose of thanking our military troops. It is a placing of the right hand on the heart and then bringing it out in a sweeping motion toward the soldier. I hope it catches on. A "Bless You".

A little more to what I really have in mind is not so much an outward gesture but an attitude of the heart. For years I have practiced a silent activity whenever I hear a siren of any type. Whether it is fire, police, or ambulance I voice a quick but silent prayer, something like this, "Dear God, someone is in trouble. Please be with them and help them in whatever way that is best for them". It just takes a moment and nobody knows about it but God and me. A "Bless You".

But maybe not. I read a story of a lady who saw a bad wreck and prayed a prayer similar to what I just described. She later heard that it was someone that she did not know but was a relative of a friend of hers. She went to see this lady when she was able to have visitors. She introduced herself to the lady and the lady said, "I remember you. You prayed for me right after the wreck happened. I want to thank you because it made me feel better when you prayed for me." The visitor was astonished and , of course, hesitant to accept such a story. Then the lady described her car in detail and also the car's direction and position in relation to the wreck.

So, perhaps those we pray for do sense that someone has "blessed" them.

Besides an actual prayer it can be just a momentary thought. You might be in a grocery store and see a cashier who is obviously having a bad day and just direct , to her, a definite thought for her wellbeing. Some call that "sending energy" It might or might not help the person directly but then again, maybe it will. It will certainly help you as you do it, and it can be done all day long as you see people about you.

The word, Namaste, is a word used in India and Nepal as a personal greeting. It can be translated in several different ways but the way that I prefer is, "The divinity within me recognizes and respects the divinity within you." I would like to adapt that into my own use, verbally with friends who would understand and non verbally toward other people about me. A "Bless You".

Many acts of kindness and respect can serve the same function. Opening a door for someone, answering the cashier who says, "Have a nice day" with a genuine smile and,"Thank you and I hope you do too!"

You can practice complimenting where it is deserved. I went into a department store several days ago and the cashier was just wonderful - concerned, accommodating, and friendly. After our transaction I said, "you know, I just wrote an article comparing the actions of a good cashier and those of a poorly trained cashier. You definitely are the "good" kind. You did everything just right!" She said, "Thank you, when you began I was hoping I would be the 'good' kind." That didn't take but a moment but she gave me the impression that it "made her day". I think it was a "Bless You".

My son lives in Miami and a friend of his, a lady who works in the Burdine's Department Store chain, would always invite my wife and me to dinner when we were in Miami. I had a favorite expression which I often used in her presence - "I appreciate ya'". Several years later she told me that she had adopted my expression in working with her fellow workers as she visited the several Burdine's stores in the state of Florida. She said that, after two years, she began to hear, every where she went in these stores, her expression and mine, "I appreciate ya'".

Perhaps you can think of some unique ways to say, "Bless You" in your own life!

CHAPTER 15: LIFE AND DEATH ARE LIKE A DRAMA

No one knows for sure what happens when we die. We feel better if we have some opinion of what happens. Different religious groups have developed various models of how to look at death. A "model" is like a theory is in science. It is an analogy that helps us to get some sort of grasp on a truth that is really too big and wonderful for our finite minds to fully understand.

So the model helps us at least to get an approximation of the truth that will help us feel more comfortable with what would otherwise be a fearful prospect. I would like to share the model of life - and death - that comforts me, knowing that it is just a model and is bound to be somewhat different from what we will know it to be after we have died.

I like to think of death, along with life, in terms of a drama. First of all, I think of everyone who is in my life in any capacity - spouse, child, parent, friend, even someone I meet once on the street, as being part of the cast of my drama. Now, here is the part that you might have trouble with, but please hear me out - I believe that all of the cast of our dramas (lives) had some sort of agreement, before we were born. We all agreed to help each other in carrying out our individual and group goals when we came to earth to put our drama into production.

Each came with his part of the drama. And each part is of tremendous importance, for without the addition of each character's contribution, however seemingly small, the drama could not proceed as planned. Have you ever witnessed a play when some prop did not work or a knock at the door did not happen as it should? An actor is supposed to say, "I wonder who that is knocking at the door?" But someone backstage missed the cue and the knock did not happen. Now what does the character say? The whole play is thrown off. Not only can the character not say his lines, but the next character now has nothing to say either. Nothing happens for long awkward moments because a simple knock did not take place at the proper time.

That is why we need to have more confidence in the timing of the Universe. Sometimes we might want the Angels (or God) to do something for us immediately because we are inpatient. But perhaps, what we are asking, without realizing it, is for the "knock on the door" to take place before its proper time according to "the Script". That, of course, if allowed to happen, would throw the whole drama off for the people whose part in our drama depends on the very thing that we are asking God to change!

Now everything in our drama is not written hard and fast into the script. There is plenty of room for improvisation. That gives us freedom to "wing it" on many occasions. I believe that some things that we do and things that happen to us do not really effect our life purpose so very much. They are learning experiences in which we find out what works and what doesn't work so well.

But then there are other times when certain things are important to our life goals. They are things that we must accomplish, people we must influence in some special way, things that we must learn or experience before we die. They are those life goals that we came to do during this life time. We will not die until those goals are accomplished. We have all heard of miracles in which people were saved from death in an accident or a usually fatal illness. Those are times when the person had not yet completed his/her life's work and so Heaven stepped in and took over. That is why I always feel, when a person dies at any age, that his life's work is finished. Otherwise he would not have died. In other words, I believe that everyone's death is written, hard and fast, into the script.

Remember also that, just as all of the parts in your drama are not starring roles. In the same way all of the parts are not "the good guys". Most plays have a villain. Now here is the hard part. That villain might be your husband or your father, or a fellow worker, or others in your drama. In the world drama you have Mother Theresa but you also have Hitler. But all of the characters, good and bad have their place in your drama. They furnish the tension through which your soul grows.

Each character helps you create your life and you help to create theirs. You might even, on occasion, be the villain in theirs. And the little lady who drives too slowly and makes you miss the green light has loved you enough to play that part for you so that you could learn a little more about yourseif from your reaction to her slowness.

That might also be a worthwhile perspective, if you can handle it, for you to have toward a less than faithful spouse or a father that beat you or embarrassed you when you were a child - he loved you enough to play that despicable part so that you might grow!

Every character's part does not run the full length of your drama, and here is the part where death becomes involved. The grand child who only lives a few days after birth - she has played her part and it is an important part. The son who dies of Aids at the young age of 33 (the same age as Jesus, by the way, when He finished all that he had come to do), the hospice worker who doesn't touch your life until just a few days before you die, yet means the world to you in that small space.

Characters come and go at different times and for varying lengths of time. Yet each is playing a key role in your drama and you, in theirs! Each made the "Knock on your door" when the proper time was there to contribute to the beautiful flow of your life's becoming.

As each person makes his exit - that whlch we call death - it is exactly as the script calls for. His/her part is done. As he enters back stage those who are behind the scenes and those who have already made their exit from your drama clap their hands and yell, "Bravo!" And when your own time comes for exit you will receive the same bouquet of flowers for the splendid part that you have played in the drama of literally thousands of people whose lives you have touched.

Chapter 16: YES, HE DOES HEAR YOU.

Martha was so close to Jesus. How could she show him her deep love? She felt that she would gladly die for him. He meant so much to her personally, to her sister and certainly to her brother, Lazarus.

She chose to honor him in the way that she knew best. She cleaned and dusted her already clean home. She carefully chose the best at the market. She would prepare the perfect meal.

The day had come. The house reflected her carefulness and, in her own special way, the love she had for Jesus. The smells that he enjoyed as he came up the walk must have assured him that he was in for a feast.

But Martha was running a little behind, just a little. It would all come out perfectly if Mary would just "pitch in" a bit - just give her a hand with the bread, and just finish the sauce for the fish.

"Why doesn't Mary check and see if her help is needed? She knows how important this is to me. How I want everything to be just perfect today so that Jesus will know. You know, I mean - how much I care for him."

"Where is she? I heard her welcome Jesus a few minutes ago. He's in there talking - I guess to Lazarus. Mary, where are you?' Oh, no - Jesus - she's bothering Jesus instead of helping me!"

"Jesus, please tell Mary to help me finish up the dinner."
(After all, I'm in here working my fingers to the bone to
show Jesus how much I love him and she's out there as
though we had all the time in the world to fix this
dinner). "Jesus, make Mary come help me! Please!"

"Martha, Martha. There are many ways to show love.
You feed me wonderful food. It gives me strength. I am
refreshed. That tells me clearly that you love me very
much. Mary listens to my every word. My words feed
her and that gives her strength. She is refreshed, and that
tells me clearly that she loves me very much also."

"I hear both of you very clearly. Her listening does not
take away from your loving preparation, and I will not
think one bit less of your wonderful love because you
were not also at my feet with open-eyed listening. Nor
do I think less of her love because she wanted to hear
my words more than she needed to look after the bread.
Do not worry. I hear the love of this whole dear family."

God is always aware that there are Marthas and Marys in
every generation. There are Jims and Roberts and
millions of other names - and each name represents a
different person. Each person is different in the way his
heart says, "I love you".

God truly accepts with great appreciation the love of
each, whether it is said with food or listening or service
or prayer or quiet devotion or with whatever voice the
heart might find with which to speak.

For there is room for everyone in the circle of God's fellowship. And no one is ever left out who desires to be there. Nor do you have to express your love with a loud voice for Him to hear you, for God always hears exceptionally well.

My Best To You Each Morning

CHAPTER 17: SOLVING LIFE'S PROBLEMS

To live life on earth is to face two things at least: Change and Problems. Most of the time we have little control over change. But problems are another thing altogether. Much of the difficulty that we have with solving problems comes from the fact that we tend to receive as our own every creature that comes our way with the label "Your Problem" written across its forehead. But I present to you that solving life's problems can be much easier than we usually think. Now, before you conclude that I am looking through rose colored glasses or over simplifying the gravity of people's problems, please hear me out.

There is, at the heart of every problem, a solution built in. It is there as surely as the problem is there. It is there as surely as there is no such thing as a bottom without a top! So, when the next problem arises in your life you need not go to books or friends for the solution. Go to the heart of the problem. That is where you will find the solution. Here is a little guide line to help:

1. Ask: "What is the problem as I see it?" Do not go further until you can answer this question clearly.

2. Then ask: "What part do I play in the problem?" If an honest answer is, "I have no part at all in the problem", then it is simply someone else's problem and not yours. The solution is clear. It is NOT A PROBLEM for you! On the other hand, if you can clearly see that you do have a part in the problem then the solution is for you to

take care of whatever you see as your part of the problem. If you do this honestly and thoroughly then your part of the problem is solved. Now, I know you are probably saying, "You didn't tell me how to take care of my part of the problem". No, but what I did was tell you how to reduce by a great percentage the number of problems you are typically dealing with every day!

3. If God or someone else is the only one that can do something about the problem then it becomes their problem and is no longer yours. If this seems "hard hearted" it is not. It is simply being realistic. There are millions of problems in the world and you can not own them all. You can only own the problems that you can do something about. All other problems are, by definition "not your problem". The rationale for this is simple. You really need to allow other people to take ownership of their problems because it is part of their growth and maturing for them to do so! You truly do them a disservice when you try to solve their problems for them. In the mean time you are hurting your own self (and perhaps your loved ones) from the stress of trying to do that which is not "doable".

4. So, to review: The solution of every problem is to see what part you play in the problem and do whatever you have it in your power to do toward its solution. When you have done that you have solved your part of the problem and it is no longer your responsibility and therefore no longer your problem, unless your part of the solution calls for further action on your part at a later time.

5. I know all of this IS over simplified and certainly the difficulty is "in the doing", but my purpose is to point out that the solution to any problem is for you to do whatever you can do toward solving it. If there is nothing you can do, then it is simply not your problem in the first place.

I think I have made that point clear, even, perhaps, to "ad nauseum!" But, hopefully, you see what I mean. Such a large amount of the stress suffered by people today comes from their attempt to take on problems that really belong to someone else. If you have ever played a sport like volley ball and the player next to you tried to play his position and yours too, then you know what I mean. Let us work on our own problems and give everybody else the chance to work on their own! And remember, it is just as unproductive to try to "play God's position" as it is to try to solve your wife's problems or your child's problems.

My Best To You Each Morning

CHAPTER 18: AN EMBLEM FOR ALL TIME

As we approach a patriotic day, such as Flag Day or Memorial Day, it is good to feel a little emotional. This poem I wrote as I thought about what might have gone through the mind of Betsy Ross, as she wondered, perhaps, just what would be the future for this nation that we call the United States of America. Listen as I read its words this morning.

On the night that Betsy Ross finished the flag, that beautiful Glory,

On that same night she committed herself in thanks to God - to be...

To be all that her fingers and eyes and talents could be

For the country that had given her such an honor.

She had no sense of what the history books would say, of course.

She did not even suspect that anyone would know what she had done,

Beyond the few patriots who had chosen her skill to be worthy.

But she somehow knew in her heart that the flag that she had fashioned

Was special beyond that which anyone there that day could sense in his fondest dream.

And so, before any eye had seen it, save herself and
God, she held its

Finished seams close to her heart and said with bowed
head...

"To Thee and to our sons and daughters I dedicate this
dear flag, Oh God.

May it always keep the salty taste of the tears of mothers
shed for sons lost in Battle.

May it show us what freedom is like as it beats Its own
rhythm to the free wind

While remaining firmly anchored to the secure mast of
principle.

Dear God, may these colors, as they float in the sunshine
of a new day

Bring the blush of patriotic love and ardor to the faces of
young and old

Who hear the bugle and the drum. With needle and
thread and cloth and heart

I offer up this banner to God and country with every
ounce of love and sincere devotion That I own.

May it always fly with respect, without embarrassment
or apology, in the eye and heart of young and old alike.

And may God bless this country for which this emblem stands, Forever and ever, Amen."

And with Betsy Ross these many years gone by, we place our own hands upon its lovely seams And say, "Amen!"

Prayer: Dear Father. Please help us to feel emotion as we think of our country. Save us from any cynicism that would lessen our sense of love and patriotism for this land of the free and home of the brave. Amen.

My Best To You Each Morning

CHAPTER 19: LIGHT INTO THIS DARK NIGHT

There is never a night so dark that there isn't at least a little bit of light somewhere in it. Evelyn's night was very dark. She could not see any light at all - not at first anyway.

She was the mother of five little children - two boys and three girls. All of them were sick at the same time and they all had the dreaded influenza. Now the "flu" in modern times would not cause much worry at all, even if all of your children had it. A few pills or a shot and it's over very quickly. But Evelyn and her kids were living in 1918, the year that the flu epidemic killed more Americans at home than died on the battle fields of Europe.

It was, indeed, a dark night for her and her very sick children. She had no husband to help her, for he had died just the year before - not of flu but from an accident at work. So Evelyn had no one at home to help and no relatives to come in to relieve her. Two of the children were very close to death and the doctor said that the next two days would "tell the story". Evelyn was not a religious person but she had always felt that God was good and loving and so she turned to Him with this simple prayer.

"Dear God. I don't know anything much about where this terrible flu came from or why it came upon us. I heard somebody say the other day that 'God sent it on us to punish us for our evil doings'. I really don't think that is so because I can't believe my kids did anything bad enough to bring this kind of thing on them. Maybe I did something bad enough but I've been thinking and, honestly God, I don't know what it would have been. So, God, I think there must be some other reason that folks are dying right and left - folks in every block losing somebody just about every day. I feel like You don't want it happening any more than we do. If there is some way that you can bring some little bitty bit of light into this dark night I would really thank you very much."

Well, the night did get somewhat less dark when the epidemic subsided. God worked with doctors and researchers to finally bring about antibiotics and vaccines that changed the word "flu" from a word that was almost synonymous with death and made it a word that, most of the time, simply means a few days at home in bed.

Now there is a dark night with the epidemic of Aids and Cancer and several other "dread" diseases. Right now it seems to be getting even darker in some parts of the world. But there is light in that darkness and there are doctors and researchers working right now to do with these dreaded ills what they have already done with flu. We have hope now that some day the words Aids and Cancer and ALS and others will mean, at worst, a few days home in a warm bed with a good book. In the mean time we can repeat with Evelyn - "Dear God...if there is some way that You can bring some little bitty bit of light into this dark night we would really thank You. Amen"

CHAPTER 20: YOU ARE SOMEONE'S LESSON

There is a call that comes in the midst of strife and suffering and difficulties of all types. It is a call to be your own self in the center of that which demands the very most of you. The call recognizes that the time of difficulty is very special. It amplifies who you are - it holds a magnifying glass over who you are and what you do and say.

As such, the magnifying situation can either be a great hindrance or a great help to whomever is in the audience of such an event. The audience, the observer, might be related directly to the event or hear about it later and indirectly by word of mouth or even by history book. But the way that you go through the fire and the way that you come out at the other end - either scorched or unscathed, or perhaps victorious in spite of being scorched - that is important. We are not saying that you must be victorious or brave or heroic.

In fact, on occasion, your greatest gift to one who observes might be to fail miserably and be willing to admit it. It might be to fail to know or do or be - and the very failing and the nature of your conduct and attitude even while failing might be the very experience which the observer needs to see in you. So, we would encourage you simply to be aware of several things.

First. When difficulties of any kind, great or small come your way, honor them and be grateful for them because whatever your being has to offer to your fellow man, it will be offered loudest and clearest at the time of difficultly - the greater the difficulty - the louder and clearer the message to the one who is to be the learner.

Secondly. Do not be concerned about avoiding difficulties. When times are pleasant, enjoy them. When times are easy, take the opportunity to rest and strengthen. But when catastrophe, problems, suffering, and such do force themselves into your expenence, do not forget that such times are very special and that they teach powerful lessons in a very concentrated and amplified way to those who are observing your life. Be happy when those days come.

Thirdly. Therefore, do not be concerned so much about whether you handle each moment successfully or well in your own eyes, for you really can not judge that. It is more important that you try to be true to yourself first of all. Then God will use your strength or weakness, your success or failure to teach the very lesson your observer needs to hear.

Lastly. Do not be overly concerned about what your life should teach. You need not know that at all. Simply know that God has built and is building lessons into your life that will come forth when their time is right and when the learner is present and ready. You do not have the slightest notion when that will be or perhaps even who the learner will be. Simply try to be your own self as well as you can and as consistently as you can. Leave the rest to God.

CHAPTER 21: SOMEWHERE OVER THE RAINBOW

This song, "Somewhere Over The Rainbow", is from the Wizard of Oz Movie. The song has been a favorite for years. Perhaps part of the reason for our loving it is that it gives us hope of a life beyond our time on earth. So, when someone close passes from us, our hope turns to the skies and beyond to Heaven. With this song in our minds and the hope of Heaven in our hearts, let us picture for a moment the scene that I describe below:

A big bird is trying very hard to fly over the rainbow!
But the rainbow seems too high as the bird flies harder and
Faster to get above the colored rays before it fades from view.

As the first brightness of the rainbow threatens to give
Way to the sunset, the great bird finally floats above the
Highest color band.

Another bird asks, "Why did you work so hard to get above a
Thing that fades away in such a short time?"

"Because it is not the length of time alone that gives value
But the beauty itself, my friend. Those few moments when I crossed above the rainbow were worth all of the effort. To see that beauty from above is next to dying"

"What a strange comparison. Isn't death something to be feared?"

"No, my friend, life is beautiful, but when you die you fly into an eternal experience more beautiful than anything ever seen on earth, more beautiful than any rainbow, and it is like going home after being away for a very long time!"

Prayer: Dear Father, help us never to fear death. Help us to trust You now and at our home going. Amen.

CHAPTER 22: A SIMPLE BALL OF TWINE

Here you see a ball of heavy twine (The twine, about an eighth of an inch thick, on a ball about two and a half inches across). There is a story behind it!

On a Saturday morning, early in March of this year, my wife and I went to yard sales. We seldom buy more than a few dollars of merchandise because there is very little that we are willing to add to the "stuff" already in our basement. Our total purchase that day was a box that my wife purchased for one dollar. It had a variety of contents, but she bought it because it had several very attractive gift bags inside.

When we got home and emptied the box, we discovered that it had this ball of twine in the bottom. I took it out and placed it on my desk.

After lunch, I decided to try out a new nylon sail that my wife had sewed for me. I have a small boat which I made of plywood in my carport. It is a little small for my weight, but I have taken it out on a local lake several times with a small trolling motor powered with the battery which I take out of the truck. Even though I made the boat as a sail boat, this was to be my maiden voyage with the sail. Just before I went out the door, I spied the ball of twine and for no reason, other than impulse, put it in my pocket.

When I got to the lake, about ten minutes away, I put the boat in the water, along with the motor, battery, sail rigging, and paddle. I used the trolling motor to get out into the middle of the lake and then began to raise the sail. Since I had a problem getting the sail fully expanded, I became distracted and did not notice that the heavy breeze was pulling one side of the boat dangerously close to the water – I did not notice, that is, until I felt some unexpected water dripping on my leg. Then, within two seconds, the whole boat was filled with water. Because I was near the rear of the boat, the front of the boat came up and over – dumping me overboard.

Ordinarily there would be only four or five people on the shore, but on this day there must have been at least seventy five people of all ages to witness my spectacular, unseasonal swim. I had on a flotation vest, so I was not at any time in danger. A young Chinese man came out immediately in a kayak and asked how he could help. I detached my trolling motor and gave it to him and he towed me to shore.

I had every expectation that the overturned boat would sink, but I forgot about the water tight pontoons that I had built on each side. The Chinese man came back out to try and tow my boat to shore, but was unable to paddle and pull at the same time. He said, "If you just had a long piece of rope, I could attach it and you could pull the boat to shore. At that very moment I remembered the ball of twine. He took it to the boat and tied it to the bow. He unrolled the ball as he came back to shore and the ball was exactly long enough to reach me on the shore. Within a few minutes I had saved the boat, paddle, motor, mast, and sail rigging. The only thing lost was the truck battery. One of the bystanders let me use her phone to call my wife to take me to get another truck battery.

Now, what is the lesson that I see in this ball of twine? I honestly believe that there are certain experiences that God would like for us to have in life, and I think that He does a bit of manipulating, at times, to see that we have those experiences. Why did someone at that yard sale throw in that ball of twine? I think, perhaps, because of a nudge from God. Why did my wife buy that particular box? Perhaps God, again. Why did I, when almost out of the door, bend over and stick the ball of twine in my pocket? According to my theory, so that I would have "rope"of exactly the right length to pull my boat in from the water.

I believe this happens often in our lives, but we just do not notice. Several days ago my wife was asked to substitute teach in a Sunday School class. The subject was to be Rahab, the harlot, from the Old Testament. She had no idea where she could get some enrichment material for that lesson. We were sitting in our living room, a place we seldom visit. She absent mindedly picked up one of the "coffee table books" which is primarily there for decorative purposes. It was called, "Women of the Bible". Sure enough, she opened to a whole chapter on Rahab, the harlot! God's nudging again?

Think on your own experience for a moment. Do you ever feel a little low and a friend calls on the phone and says, "I was just thinking about you and thought I would call and see how you are getting along?" Do you ever have a door open up just after another has closed?

Why did God nudge someone to put this little ball of twine in a box weeks ago? Was it to save my boat? Perhaps. Was it to furnish me with a topic for this morning's devotional? Perhaps, again. Or could it be that the nudge of God on that far off day might have been, not so much about the boat but so that you, on this day, might take a brief moment to remember again that God loves us all enough to take time to make a few nudges that might bring about something helpful in our lives. If that is the case, He also nudged a Chinese man, a lady who offered her telephone, and who knows how many others just to bring us a blessing this Sunday morning.

CHAPTER 23: THE PRINCIPLE OF "GRADUALIZATION"

Well, here is my ball of twine again! No, I am not going to tell the story of another overturned boat! But this ball of twine reminds me of a story that I heard a few days ago that I want to share with you this morning. It is about the first bridge that was ever built at Niagara Falls.

Back in the 1800's, the only way to get from Canada to the USA, or vice versa, in the Niagara Falls area, was to go across on a ferry boat. A Canadian gentleman, named William Merritt, dreamed of some day building a bridge across that chasm. He got his chance in about 1848 when he received permission from both countries to build a railroad suspension bridge in the falls area. Two companies were formed, one on each side, to attempt the project. I say "attempt" because many people thought it could never be done. After all, it was a span of 800 feet!

The companies hired a young engineer, Charles Ellet, to tell them how to go about it. Mr. Ellet thought long and hard about the situation and he decided that the best way to begin was with a kite! So he advertised a kite flying contest. The first person to successfully fly and land a kite from one cliff to the other would receive a $5.00 prize! (I am sure that $5.00 seemed like much more money in those days than it would now).

On the first day of the contest, no one succeeded. On the second day, a 16 year old, Homan Walsh, took his kite over to the Canadian side and successfully landed on the

New York side. The kite cord was immediately tied to a tree and a heavier cord was tied to the other end. The heavier cord was then pulled across the chasm and secured. Then a rope was tied on and pulled across, followed by a steel cable. Finally a heavier cable was brought over and each end was secured to a wood tower on each cliff bank.

A sort of large wicker basket with two chairs was hung from the cable on pulley wheels, so that it could be drawn across both ways with ropes. Two people could be transported at one time for $1.00 per person round trip.

A little later this was upgraded to a walking bridge about three feet wide. People were allowed to walk each way for 25 cents round trip.

Finally the foot bridge was replaced by a two level suspension bridge with the top level transporting a railroad track and the lower level a regular road for pedestrians and horse drawn carriages. It was the first such railroad suspension bridge in the world!

This whole process I have called "gradualization". I am sure there is a more scientific name but I do not know it. The principle is, to begin small and, with patience, persistence, and expectation, to finally accomplish something of great worth.

My first experience of this principle was when I was six years old. My father helped me take small balsa wood sticks, cut and glue them together over a set of plans, and with patience, persistence, and expectation we built a model airplane that would actually fly!

I have used this principle all of my life since that day. I have built more model airplanes, boats, musical instruments, and even added a room to my house using this very same principle. No doubt the house that you live in was built on the principle of "gradualization". Builders began with one 2x4 and nailed it to another 2x4. This was repeated until a wall was completed. Then three more walls were done in the same way and all four walls were joined together. Basically, with patience, persistence, and expectation, a few pieces of 2x4s became your lovely home!

Now God, who taught us this principle, uses it every day! He applies it differently to different parts of His creation. He takes a bean seed and, with patience, persistence, and expectation, produces a plant with beans in two months. He takes a redwood seed and in the same fashion produces trees that will live for hundreds of years.

But, when he works with mankind, he works with us, not for 70 or 90 years but for eternity! There was a popular saying a few years ago that "God ain't finished with me yet!" While it is true, I would like to rephrase that to be "God has just begun working with you and me".

If we ever find ourselves thinking, "my life is almost over", then what we need is a new perspective. Our lives are just beginning! God is using the principle of "gradualization" with us. When we do leave this earth to go to Heaven, we are not going to hibernate like a bear or spend our time sitting on a cloud for a million years! We are going to continue growing and learning and developing – just like that bridge developed from that one piece of kite cord. Who knows but that our lives, thus far, are only the "kite cord beginning" of our eternal existence! I truly believe that it is!

If you ever begin to feel down because you think that you haven't accomplished much in your life, remember that God is practicing gradualization with you! He will patiently and persistently use all of eternity to bring us to where he wants us to be.

So, do not be too hard on yourself. Try not to be discouraged. Whatever is weak about you, God will strengthen for you in His time. It is just the "unfinished" part of you! If this life is just the "kite cord phase", God has eternity to bring us to what He wants us to be. Right now, I believe that He is quite happy with the fact that our kite cord has been tied to a "tree somewhere on the other side!"

CHAPTER 24: THE THREE PEOPLE WHO USE YOUR TOOTH BRUSH

Several weeks ago my wife and I were visiting a friend and she said that she had left her hearing aid for repairs and the "loaner" wasn't working right. I said, "Try mine." She did and said, "This works fine!" So I said, "Let me try your loaner". I did and it worked fine for me. So we traded hearing aids for a day or two. I said, "Next we will be using each other's tooth brush!" We all had a good laugh out of that. It reminded me that I once gave a graduation address entitled, "The Three People Who Use Your Tooth Brush". It was similar to but not exactly what I want to talk about this morning.

I do not wish to be irreverent when I say this, but, if God had a tooth brush, there would be three people using that tooth brush – God, the Father, God, the Son, and God, the Holy Spirit.

In a like sense, there are many people who use your tooth brush. You might be a father or mother and at the same time be a son or daughter. You might be a doctor, sales person, or housewife. You might at the same time be a friend, a gardener, a jogger, etc. and you have a little different function with each role. But all of these come out of who you are. They all use the same toothbrush! I would like to refer to three other people who use your tooth brush and show how these relate to God.

The first person who uses your tooth brush is "You - the Forgiver". God said, "I was in Christ reconciling the world unto myself (forgiving the world) and have given to each of you the ministry of reconciliation (or forgiving). Christ said, "Those whom you forgive on earth will be forgiven in Heaven."

One of the biggest problems of some of the people who come in and out of our lives every day is the inability to forgive themselves. They might believe that God forgives but they can not get the full relief of that forgiveness because they can not quite forgive themselves for something they did or did not do. If only I had not........ Or, if only I had done this or that. That is where you come in. Any time you sense that someone is walking with a heavy load of guilt on their shoulders, if they are willing to share it with you, you can work a miracle by affirming that God does forgive and showing that you are confident of that forgiveness and that you respect and believe in them in spite of what they did or did not do.

Forgiveness is like CPR. Even a heart surgeon can not do CPR on himself. It takes another person outside of himself. Often it takes another person to bring about a person's acceptance of forgiveness.

The second person who uses your tooth brush is "You the Blesser". In Bible times there were many stories that showed the importance of the blessing of a child by his parents. One of the functions of the Holy Spirit is to help us feel the blessings of our Father, God. But it is a basic need of every human being to feel the blessing or approval of their parents, family, and spouse.

There are many people that you brush shoulders with every day who never once heard their father say, "You did a good job, Son!" They never heard their mother say, in so many words, "I love you!" They never heard their brother or sister say, "I'm proud to be your brother!" Perhaps they feel that, down deep, their spouse thinks that they would have done better if they had "married the other guy"! There are lots of people all around you who have never felt blessed by the significant people in their lives. Surprisingly, you can fulfill that function. Listen for statements like, "I never do anything right!", or, "I could never do anything like that!" or, "There I go again! - I always mess up!" These are often the words of someone who has not fully received the blessing or respect and trust by the important people in his or her life. By affirming this person every chance you get, over time, you can fill in the blessing they missed getting before.

Well, the third person who uses your tooth brush is "You, the Brother/Sister". Christ is often depicted as our brother. He lifted up the example of being a brother and sister to each other. As we get to know each other in church or at work or in neighborhoods, we begin to feel the needs of each other. Especially with older folks we see the changes in our lives that leave us vulnerable. Loss of spouse, loss of family members, loss of health, loss of the ability to drive, loss of vision. All of these changes and many others make us need each other in small ways and great ways. When we hear of these needs we can be such a tremendous help to each other by just caring. Offering to do the little things and the big things that will help them live their lives just a little bit better and boost their spirits – that is being a brother or sister to them, and it will make a difference.

There are many people who use your tooth brush, but none are more important than You - the Forgiver, You - the Blesser, or You - the Brother/Sister/Helper!

CHAPTER 25: OUR INFLUENCE

I was shopping in a super market yesterday and, over the loud speaker, I heard a song - "Sunshine on my shoulder makes me happy!". It was, of course, John Denver! For a minute or two I almost forgot where I was. I saw John's face, his hair, his guitar. I had several minutes of sheer joy as I remembered other songs and TV specials I had seen with John and his care free, thoughtful songs of roads and mountains, and fresh oceans and skies. I found myself wishing that I could bless people like that. Here I am in a grocery store, 14 years after John died in that tragic plane crash, and he is still blessing me! Then it dawned on me, almost like an answer to my wish. I CAN do that! We ALL can do that!

Everyone who lives a while among other folks has such a far reaching influence as that. There will be moments, when you are gone or even now, when someone close to you – perhaps a daughter or son - will be walking in a store. They will see a brand of cereal or a magazine on a shelf and they will say to themselves, "Dad always liked that!" or, "That was Mom's favorite!" And they will have those few moments of sheer delight that I had with John Denver. They will see your hair, your face, your smile, and will remember some loving incident with you that will warm their heart. The sound of a song can take me back to when I was on my mother's lap and she sang it to me. The sight of a pot bellied stove puts me back into the hours I enjoyed in my grandmother's parlor. When we sing a certain song in church, my wife and I always look at each other and smile, for it is the favorite song of one of the deacons in my first church pastorate 48 years ago. Even to hear the title of the song allows us to enjoy again the times we had with that good man.

So, you and I, we have the capacity built in. God made us that way! To illustrate the point, on the same Wednesday that I heard John Denver, we took a neighbor to a doctor's appointment. On the way home our neighbor pointed to a certain house and said, "Mrs.B. lived there, did you know her at First Baptist?" My wife answered in the affirmative. The neighbor continued, "Her husband taught my brother in Sunday School and also in public school, probably 70 years ago. When her husband died, I sent Mrs. B. a note expressing how much her husband had meant to my brother in those days. Years later Mrs. B. called me on the phone and said, "I was looking through my old letters yesterday and came across the note you sent me years ago when Bill died. It means so much to me now just reading it again. I just wanted you to know."

Now, just think about the life cycle of that blessing! Mr. B. blessed my neighbor's brother. My neighbor blessed Mrs. B. with a note. Years later Mrs. B. blessed my neighbor with a phone call. Then several years later our neighbor blessed my wife and me by retelling the story. Now I am telling you! All from the original blessing of a school teacher being himself in class in a loving, caring way!

We all are doing that sort of thing every day. By the way, I really think that Heaven is set up in such a way that, somehow, John Denver knows that he blessed me on Wednesday morning at 10:00. I believe that Mrs. B. and her brother know that they blessed us on the way home from the doctor. I believe that you and I will some day be aware of how the loving things we say and do today will keep on blessing other folks long after we go to our reward.

My Best To You Each Morning

CHAPTER 26: THE PRIVILEGE OF NAMING THINGS

When I was a junior in high school, my parents gave me my first car. It was an American Bantam convertible. This was in the year 1950 and the car was a 1941 model. It was made at the beginning of World War II and only 800 of these cars were made before the factory was shut down because of the war. I recently saw a model like mine in a car museum and if I had kept the car all these years it would be worth over $85,000.

But back to my story. It was a small car and, on occasions when I ran out of gas at home, I would get on my bike and go to a gas station with a quart milk bottle and get enough gas for me to be "back in business"! I decided to name my car. I painted the name in small letters on the driver's side door. "Hadacol"was the name. You might remember that it was the name of a health medicine in the 1950's that was supposed to be loaded with vitamins. My mother did not much like the name and asked why on earth I chose the name "Hadacol". I can't believe what I said. My answer was, "Well, I hada call it something!" My mother was wise enough to respect my right to name it. After all, it was MY car.

In the Bible – Genesis 2:19 – the story is told that, after God created all of the animals, he brought them to Adam. Whatever Adam called it, that was the name that it would be known by! Most of us are familiar with that story. But perhaps we are not as familiar with another "naming gift"that God gave to man – and to woman. It is the unique privilege of naming every event that happens to us! We have the right to call each event a "curse"or a "blessing"!

We see this gift demonstrated in the story of Job. Almost every bad thing that could happen, happened to Job. But I have just stepped beyond bounds by calling these things "bad". Only Job had the privilege of naming these events. His friends tried to tell him that they were punishments from God. "If I were you, Job, I would call it a curse!" Even Job's wife said, "Job, why don't you just curse God and die!".But Job would only say, "even if God kills me, I will still trust him!" In other words, Job was saying, "Because I trust God, I am going to call everything that has happened to me a "blessing". I am going to expect some good to come out of all my troubles".

What are the bad things that happen to us today? Illness, financial distress, loss of loved ones, spiritual doubts – the same things that came to Job. But God gives us the privilege of calling each thing a "curse"or a "blessing". Many people have gone through cancer, aids, accidents, etc. and afterward said, "It was the best thing that ever happened to me. It did not seem so at the time, but, as a result of what I went through, my whole life was changed for the better! God used my trouble to really be a blessing to my life!"

Is there anything that is making your life difficult right now? Someone has said that, "most of our unhappiness comes from our unwillingness to accept 'what is'" In other words, we want this or that circumstance to be different. We want our spouse or a child or a grand child to be different than what they are. We want our bodies to quit hurting or be well. It might even be that we are not happy because we have spiritual doubts. But many who have gone through what they called "a dark night of the soul"have been able to say, as doubting Thomas must have said, "God accepted me in my doubts and made me even stronger".

So, what I am suggesting is, let us look at our lives, just as they are, and say, "Lord, I thank you for my life, just as it is. I choose to call it a blessing. Please use any of it to teach me, to change me, or to help me be more what you want me to be. Help me to be able to name each thing that you allow me to experience – a "Blessing".

My Best To You Each Morning

CHAPTER 27: TROMBONE PLAYERS

The story goes that a man who played trombone in a Vaudeville pit orchestra, years ago, wanted to get away for the week end. He asked a friend if he would "sit in for him" for three shows at $5.00 each show. The friend said, "how can I do that. I can't play the trombone?" The player said, "that's no problem. You show up with my trombone. When the music starts you watch the other trombone player. When he puts his trombone up to his mouth you do the same. However he moves his slide you do that too. Don't blow or make a sound. The other guy will carry the tune and nobody will know the difference.

"That sounds fine to me", said the friend. So he showed up at the proper time, introduced himself to the other trombone player, and waited. The leader lifted his baton, the music started, and both men watched each other, and watched, and watched. It seems that both trombone players had hired substitutes.

Now, that brings me to something that happened one morning in our church orchestra. There are three trombone players, playing three parts. A young man plays the first part which consists of the higher notes. I play the second part, which is similar to the first part but plays notes in the middle register and usually in harmony with the first part. The other gentleman plays the bass trombone part which is made up of lower notes like a tuba plays.

In our performance that particular morning, we were playing a special piece in which the first and second players had a very important solo. We played this solo in unison and had always played it pretty well. But the director wanted the solo to sound even stronger, so he asked the bass player to copy the solo onto his music so that he could play it with us and make it even stronger.

So the bass player copied the solo. We were all ready to come out strong. But somehow, though it had never happened before, the first trombone player miscounted and thought we had one more measure before we were to play.. I also made the same mistake. The bass player was the only one who came in and played the solo. The first trombone player and I sat there looking at each other just like we were a couple of hired substitutes!

I would add this application to my story. The first and second trombone players thought that everything was depending on them for the solo passage, but, as it turned out, there was a back up.

Many of us think that we are actually more important than we are. We grow older and we become nervous, thinking that, if we get sick or die our job will not be done, our children will suffer, our wives will be devastated. But I have come to believe that God has backups even for us. I am not really trying to say that we would not be missed. I am sure that we would be. But I have known many families that have done quite well when a father or mother have died early in life. In my own case, I lived much of my childhood with a single mother. I think I turned out well because God had a backup. Our extended family of aunts, uncles, and cousins took up the slack. So, all that I am saying is that we should live as long as we can, do the best that we can, but have faith that God will have a backup for us if, indeed, we must leave life sooner than we planned. If we do have that confidence, we will live our life more confidently.

Prayer: Father, help us to live confidently, joyfully, and with full assurance that You have back up plans for all of us. Amen.

My Best To You Each Morning

CHAPTER 28: A PERSPECTIVE ON DEATH

I recently went through a time of indecision about medicine. My doctor wanted me to take a statin drug for my cholesterol problem but I had heard about certain dangers connected with statins. So, I took them for a while, left them off, took a natural remedy for a while, then finally decided to go back to the statins.

My doctor finally said, Mr. Hancock, you need to stop spending so much energy over this. First of all, your chances of dying from cholesterol are much higher than any dangers from a statin. But secondly, we are all going to die from something!

Well, I thought long and hard about his last statement and concluded that, in reality, we spend far too much energy in worrying about the whole subject of dying.

When I was younger and felt some ache or pain I would have a degree of anxiety about death and think, well, I hope that I can live long enough to see my boys graduate from high school. Now that I am 76 years old, I find that many of my friends worry simply because people my age are either dying, discovering the beginning of a terminal illness, or showing signs of Alzheimer's disease. So I would like to offer a few helpful perspectives on death for your consideration.

I would start with my doctor's reminder that we will all die of something. That is a given. With that fact out of the way, there are only two things to worry about, when and how. If you are a person of religious faith, you would agree that, beyond observing reasonable rules of good health, we have little to do with the when. So a good perspective on the when is two fold. Here I am speaking to my own generation primarily. Our children are grown, we have already lived long enough that anything else is just icing on the cake. Secondly, and this is true for any age, our alternative to living in fear of when is just to live with awareness , meaning, and gratitude during each moment of our lives, no matter how long that might be.

So, that leaves the only thing to worry about is the how of our death. Well, outside of living as healthy a lifestyle as possible there isn't much we can do about the how either. But there is a great deal that we can do about the worry.

As near as I can determine, the how will be one of three types: 1. Sudden death , like a heart attack, aneurysm, or fatal accident. 2. A brief illness , perhaps in the hospital. 3. A lengthy, debilitating illness of mind, body, or both.

If I were to ask you which of these you would prefer NOT to experience, it would probably be the last. So let us consider that first. How can we avoid worrying about a devastating illness that is expensive and which tears up the lives of our spouse and/or our children? Well, here is my perspective on that.

This came to my attention just a few days ago. As a hospice volunteer, I was helping a wife reposition her husband in his bed. It dawned on me that, in this man's condition, his wife will probably have to do everything for him, just as if he were a baby, for the rest of his life. But then, immediately I had this thought. Why would I want to deprive this woman of what could be one of the most meaningful experiences of her long marriage, perhaps even of her whole life. My concern for what she was about to have to suffer was, of course, understandable.

But would not my reasoning be comparable to a mother saying to her daughter, Dear, I do want you to have children but I certainly don't want you to have to go through that awful period of babyhood. You will have dirty diapers and baby bottles and waking up at all times of the night. You will even have to carry the baby everywhere he goes. Now, I just don't want you to have to go through all of THAT. The daughter would be justified in saying, Mother, THAT is one of the most important parts of having a family! Why would you want me to miss THAT?'

So, I face the possibility that , either myself or my wife might have a lengthy and debilitating death. My perspective for that possibility is, that if that happens there will be value in that outcome for all involved: for myself, for my wife and family, for all of my friends, and even for the medical profession. So, perhaps the desire to wish away such an experience is unwise and unmerited. It certainly does not deserve my worry, beyond whatever reasonable preparation I can afford, such as long term insurance.

The second possibility would be the one that, perhaps, most of us would pick. A brief illness would give you time to adjust to the outcome, time to get your business in order, time to make suggestions for your funeral if you are so inclined, and most importantly, time to exchange important words with your family and friends. The period of anticipation would be short and whatever pain could likely be controlled. The expense, inconvenience, and anxiety of your family and your self would be minimized. If that is the way it happens then there is nothing to worry about in that.

The first possibility that I mentioned, sudden death, might be the first choice for a few but not for most of us. We would fear the possibility that we might die without having the opportunity to say a final I love you to our family. You might dread the idea of having to leave all of the lose ends of your personal and family business for your family to have to deal with. This scenario, of course, would have the advantage of minimal medical expense and a minimal period of anticipatory anxiety.

But my perspective on this, I think, will lessen the worry considerably. At least I have found it to be so. My secret to minimizing the worry here is to do before hand everything that you fear you might not have the opportunity to do otherwise.

I will tell you briefly how I have handled this. First, of course, I do what I can, health wise, to avoid that outcome. Secondly, since I have seen how difficult it is for families to plan a memorial service when they are trying to do it just as they feel the deceased would desire, I have left fairly detailed suggestions as to music and scripture and have even included my own little insert of what I want to be sure is said.

I have written notes to my wife and children, expressing my love and appreciation for their contribution to my life. I even update this every several years. I also included my will, my living will giving directions concerning life support preferences, and a power of attorney document. And all of this is in one central folder that my wife is aware of. In my case, my wife is the business and finance expert and she has left detailed guidelines of our finances , but in cases where one spouse would be totally in the dark then this knowledge and practice should be equally shared between the two.

So, briefly, my perspective on death is this. Live each day in a meaningful way in case your death is sudden and without warning. Do whatever preparation you can do that will minimize your family's trauma in case your death is of that nature. The result for yourself is that your worry will be greatly decreased.

Do not build up in your mind a scenario of the awfulness of the possibility of your prolonged and degenerating death. No one can say with certainty that such an occurrence would not be a life enriching experience for all involved. So, trust whatever deity you believe in to make a decision that will be for the highest good of all.

Lastly, if you are one of those whose warning is short but still adequate for all that you need to do before departing, then consider yourself blessed and be grateful.

In all cases, try to replace any burdensome worry that you now carry with some sort of positive perspectives similar to these that I have suggested. You will find that your journey will be much more pleasant and, more than likely, your days will be prolonged as a result.

CHAPTER 29: ZERO SHOPPING DAYS 'TIL CHRISTMAS

How times have changed when it comes to Christmas shopping! We often begin our shopping plans even before Thanksgiving, seeing signs of Christmas competing for our attention with Halloween costumes and candy "give aways".

But I remember a Christmas when I discovered that all of my shopping days had gotten away from me, and I would like to share that story with you.

It was in 1948. My mother and I had moved from Savannah, Georgia, USA, to Jacksonville, Florida. She had just married my step father and we rented a small bungalow in North Jacksonville. That summer I got a job working in a grocery store on the weekends and my step father began working as a 7 up drink delivery man. I helped him on his truck during the week.

That fall I began high school and my step father was able to borrow some money from his mother and he purchased the first quick car wash facility that we had ever seen. The concept of quick car washing was new at the time. The "Jiffy Car Wash" consisted of a home made blower with duct work arms that engulfed the car like a giant octopus.

The car wash staff consisted of my step father who managed, my mother who took the money, and myself, who, after school and on week ends, vacuumed the cars and kept them pulled up in the line of operation. I learned to drive in the process. In addition we kept three or four stout men who did the actual washing and drying.

The price of a car wash was $1.00, and we were barely able to meet expenses during the week. Our profit was made if and when we had a fair weather Saturday and Sunday. If it rained either day we would just hope for a better week end next week.

Holidays were usually an extra help to the company pocket book, and this first Christmas we were hoping to "get a little bit ahead". All of our energy was put into getting the workers committed to being there on Christmas Eve, which that year was Saturday, and in hoping that the weather would hold up. If all went well we would show a little profit for the year and pay off a few bills.

But in the hustle and bustle of preparing for our big car wash week end, we had given absolutely no thought to Christmas shopping. Now, I know that is hard for you to imagine in this day and time, but we had no television, we did not take the newspaper and so Christmas advertising was just not a big item in our lives.

So, at the end of Christmas Eve, we happily paid off the work crew and found that we had about $100 profit. It had been a very good day indeed! We even decided to let everyone off the next day - Christmas!

But it dawned on us that we had not even done any Christmas shopping for each other. We wondered if

anything would still be open at 7:00 P.M. On Christmas
Eve. There were no Walmarts or K Marts in those days.
We drove uptown and found two stores open - a pawn
shop and a drug store. In the drug store we got a box of
face powder for my mother and some Old Spice shaving
lotion for my step father. Then we went to the pawn
shop and we purchased the very first fishing rod and reel
that I ever owned.

The next day, Christmas Sunday, was cold and blustery
with a threat of rain. But I was so anxious to try out my
rod and reel that my folks got up early and we went to
the nearby Trout River and rented a row boat. The only
bait we had was the single shiny minnow lure that we
had purchased with the rod combo.

There was not a chance in the world that we would catch
a fish. But my folks were giving me the gift of my first
fishing experience and it was memorable. We almost
froze during the two hours that we hoped for a fish to
strike, but nothing happened. Nothing, that is, until a
hungry pelican saw what he thought was to be his
Christmas dinner and swooped down to ingest my pretty
shiny lure.

For several minutes we tried desperately to disengage
the grapple hook from the jaws of the frantic bird. His
large wings beat against our attempts to be charitable.
Finally, we were able to hold him still long enough to
remove the hook, and the bird flew away with many
angry bird - words of insults and cursing.

We caught no fish that Christmas but it was the beginning of a life time of fishing enjoyment for me. Even more important it reflected how much enjoyment family love can create even amid meager resources. On that Christmas day we saw the birth of a memory that is still alive sixty years later - alive with the glow of love and joy and the sense of how very little of the world's goods it really takes to produce a Happy Christmas.

Prayer: Dear Father. We say this every Christmas but we really do mean it. Please help us to remember the true meaning of Christmas - Love - Your Love for us, our Love for You, and our Love for each other. Amen.

CHAPTER 30: TWO EXAMPLES OF SYNCHRONICITY

I consider the two events that follow to be examples of what Carl Jung, the Swiss Psychologist, called Synchronicity. Synchronicity is when two or more events happen in a meaningful manner but are not causally related. And their happening is under circumstances that go beyond what could be expected from "coincidence". There are different ways that people try to explain synchronistic events. I prefer to think that, at least in some of these cases, God, the Universe, Destiny, or whatever you might call a power beyond human power, takes some part in influencing events in order to bring together two individuals for the benefit of one or both. I believe that my story illustrates two such interventions. But you can be your own judge of that.

I am not sure when Bob (I am changing his name to respect his privacy) graduated from Stetson University but I think it was 1952 or 53. I was a freshman in 1951-52 and Bob was a senior. Bob was something of a superstar to Stetson and especially to the people of Deland, Florida. He was a music major with a wonderful voice and personality, and whenever he had a concert there was standing room only and standing ovations were always the norm. I was a freshman with very little money who wanted desparately to become a member of the glee club.

It was required that I have a white Palm Beach suit, which was the uniform of the glee club. Such a suit would have cost about $60.00, which was a lot of money, over a week's wages, in those days. So I went to the bulletin board in the music school and there I saw a Palm Beach suit in (almost) my size for about $10.00. It had Bob Sturgis' name and address. I could afford that. (And I probably thought if I got his suit I could even sing better). I called him first and then went by his house to buy the suit.

About a week later I had gone home for the week end (to Jacksonville) and was on the way back on Sunday night with two girl students who also lived in Jacksonville. As we drove through Palatka, which was about 50 miles from home and about the same distance from Stetson, my 36 Ford quit running, just as if it were out of gas. I knew it was not out of gas because I had filled its tank before leaving Jacksonville. But nothing was open but a little grocery store, so I called a buddy at Stetson and he came the 50 miles (a real buddy indeed) and took us back to school.

The next day I set out to go back to "be with" my car, though I had no idea at all what I would do. I walked to the highway and began to "thumb" for a ride. Along came Bob. He recognized me from having sold the suit to me (God's first provision?) and asked where I was going. I said, "Palatka" and he said, "hop in! I'm going that way." As we talked I told him how the car had stopped just like it was out of gas. He said, "Don, I had a 36 Ford and it did the same thing. Do you have a pair of pliers?" "Yes," I said, "it's the only tool I have in the car except a tire wrench". He told me that it was probably the mechanical fuel pump.

He told me where to look for it and to take out the two bolts and take off the pump. It would have a lever with a cup the size of a thimble and an operating rod sticking into the cup. He said to take off the pump and find an old pipe tobacco can and break off a piece of the tin about an inch long and three eighths of an inch wide with the pliers and fold it twice and put that as a shim into the cup. The operating rod had just worn down too much to operate the pump effectively and the shim will take up the slack.

Well, he let me out, I immediately found the tin can (did God have a "hand" in that also?) and within about 45 minutes I was ready to try it out. My 36 Ford purred like a kitten. Now what are the chances of a fellow coming along who recognized me and was going past Palatka and had had a 36 Ford that just happened to have a worn fuel pump operating rod that he had fixed himself instead of taking it to the shop?

Well, Bob graduated and I lost track of him. I felt that I would always be grateful to him for selling me his suit and especially for his coming to my rescue. But, now fast forward about 30 years. I had graduated from Stetson, gone to Seminary in preparation for the ministry, met my wife, and had gotten my Th.M.degree with special preparation for the Chaplaincy. I graduated in 1960. No chaplain's position was open so I accepted an Associate Pastorate in Louisville, Kentucky. Then I was a pastor for several years until a Chaplain's position opened at a facility for mentally disabled persons in Augusta, Georgia.

After 13 years in that position, I was getting pretty "burned out". I and two other Chaplains went to a Chaplains' Conference that happened to be meeting in Atlanta. I think the year was about 1983. During that conference I became very aware that I needed someone to talk with. The night session looked pretty boring so I looked in the newspaper and saw that there was a movie I wanted to see playing in a suburban theatre way across town. "Perhaps some distraction might help," I thought. Since I had come to Atlanta with another Chaplain, I took a bus all the way across Atlanta to the Theatre.

After the movie I still felt really down. Coming out of the Theatre I saw a guy that looked familiar. I went closer and said, "Bob Sturgis?" "Yes!" "Well, I'm Don Hancock from Stetson. Do you remember the time you picked up a fellow with a broke down 36 Ford, and you.....etc. ?" "Yes, I remember you, Don! Well, let's talk Where's your car?" "Well, it's like this, I came on a bus and.....etc."

So for the second time Bob Sturgis gave me a ride when I was broken down. He took me to my hotel and we sat and talked for a couple of hours at least. When he left he had given me some more hints about how to fix what was "broken down". Now what are the chances of two people in a city the size of Atlanta choosing the same movie at the other end of town at the same time? It certainly seems to me that, again, God had put His hand into my life and brought the very best person to pick me up and give me exactly what I needed to get going again.

Prayer: Help us, Father, to know that you are even more involved in our lives than we are. Help us to trust that you want the very best for each of us. Amen.

My Best To You Each Morning

CHAPTER 31: HALLOWEEN REVISITED

In 1940, I was a seven year old living in Miami, Florida. My mother was married again but my real father was also living in Miami. I would visit him on occasion and stay with him for a few days in his small apartment in back of his sign painting shop.

On Halloween of that year, I was staying with him for the week end. It so happened that there was some sort of community center just across the street from my Dad's shop, and they had advertised on a big sign that there would be a Halloween Party for all of the kids in the neighborhood that night. It said that there would be candy and cake and games and movies. I was really looking forward to going, but I did not have any kind of a costume. My Dad helped me make a pair of "Vampire Teeth" out of cardboard and I was quite content to let that be my costume.

When the time for the party came, I put in my "teeth" and crossed the street to the entrance of the center. There was a group of guys a little older than me standing there and they began to laugh and point their fingers and say things like, "Boo!" and "Ain't he scary? Oh, Oh!" I was immediately humiliated and ran back to my father's shop. No amount of persuading on his part would make me go back to the party.

Now, fast forward to 1985. My wife and I and our two sons were already living in Augusta, Georgia. My youngest son had chosen to attend a college in Miami, and on his 18th birthday we escorted him down to his new school. Seven years later, in 1992, I returned to Miami to take him a new car and bring his old car back to Augusta. This visit happened to be on Halloween!

My son, Dean, told me that there was to be a big, outdoor Halloween party in his neighborhood and he wanted us to go. I immediately protested that we did not have costumes. He said, "No problem. I have a couple of friends down the hall who are entertainers. I am sure they can fix us up with something!" As it turned out, the two young men provided us with two complete Pirate outfits, complete with swords, turbans, and eye patch. After supper we dressed up and went to the most fabulous party I have ever seen. There was all sorts of entertainment, food, and music. There were guys walking on stilts in monster sized costumes as clowns, animals, and witches. It was one of of those nights that I will always remember.

As we walked back to Dean's apartment, I told him the story of my first Halloween in Miami. I felt very strongly the contrast between that time of humiliation and this wonderful, happy event that night. Then I put it this way. "Dean, it is almost as though Miami was sorry for its previous actions and the city was making amends, 52 years later – redeeming the first sad situation with an almost overdose of warm friendship tonight!" He was so taken with the contrast that he shared the story with many of his friends over the coming years. It became a part of our family history. Now, 71 years after the first Halloween and 19 years after the second Halloween, we still talk about the night that "Miami redeemed itself!"

Now, how does this story apply to us today? It occurs to me that one of the main purposes of God has always been the righting of wrongs, the making whole of that which is incomplete. It is what the word, "redemption"is all about. It is what Paul was thinking about when he mentioned the redemption of time. Time has a way of moving our lives along from day to day. And in that moving we find that we leave things undone that we should have done and some things are done that we wish had not been done. We find ourselves regretting these short comings. We find ourselves wishing that we could some how go back and do certain things differently if we just had another chance. That is what God is about. That is what He has ALWAYS been about! I spoke of Miami as though it had consciously been sorry that it had treated 7 year old Donnie Hancock poorly and made sure they did better the second time. That rationale was, of course, all in my own mind. But I think that it does illustrate what God is about!

In Revelations 7:17 it says, "God shall wipe away all tears from their eyes." I really think that is saying more than just those words imply. I think that it means that, some day, God is going to gather up all of the missed opportunities that we regret right now. He will give us another chance to fulfill them. I think that all of the things that we have done that we are ashamed of – things that hurt others and things that hurt ourselves – these things we will have another chance to put right. In every area of our lives that we now see lack and incompleteness, God will give us the rest of our eternal lives to "get it right" with His help! The way that God will "wipe away the tears from our eyes" will be that He will remove all of the reasons that we ever cried in the first place!

So, just as I felt, that second Halloween in Miami, that all things had been "put right", you and I will also feel, when we get back to our Heavenly home, that everything – EVERYTHING - has been "put right"by our Heavenly Father's love!

CHAPTER 32: THE LITTLE BOY ON VALENTINE'S DAY*

Little Chad was a quiet, shy little boy. Just before Valentine's day, he told his mother that he wanted to make a Valentine for all of his classroom and neighborhood friends. She really did not like the idea, because she had noticed how the neighborhood children seemed to ignore Chad as they walked to school each day. They talked among themselves while Chad walked alone. But she went ahead and bought paper, glue, and crayons for his project. Every night, for three weeks, Chad carefully made individual cards for each of his friends.

On Valentine's Day, Chad was so excited. He carefully put all of the cards in a bag and ran out the door to school. His mother made his favorite cookies and some cocoa when it was time for him to come home. She was sure that he would be down hearted with the way the children received his cards. She felt that he would probably get very few cards in return.

Sure enough, when she heard the children walking down the street, they were all talking and laughing among themselves but Chad was walking all by himself. The mother expected to hear Chad burst into tears the moment he came into the house. She saw that Chad's arms were empty and she had to try to hold back her own tears.

"Mommy has some cookies and cocoa for you", she said.

Chad hardly heard her words. He just marched right on by, All he could say was, "Not a one! Not a single one!.

Her heart sank.

Then he added with a broad smile, "I didn't forget a single one of my friends! Not a single one!"

To me, this story is sort of a modern day allegory. The boys and girls are like many of the people in the world today – they are so wrapped up in their own lives and relationships that they seldom think of God. We might think that we put God first in our lives, but in reality, we are more concerned with ourselves than with God.

The mother is like the religious leaders down through the centuries. She was loving but she was mostly concerned about the little boy being hurt. She probably felt like giving the thoughtless children a good spanking. She probably felt like saying to her son, "forget about those thoughtless, selfish kids! They don't deserve to be your friend!"

The religious leaders - the Prophets, Priests, Preachers, and Evangelists – down through history, have emphasized the negatives that they believed about God. They have preached about God's wrath, His jealousy, and His judgment, almost as if they were trying to protect God from being rejected.

The little boy, of course, is like God. The mother expected him to feel disappointed, rejected, misused, and resentful. He didn't! She probably felt like giving the boys and girls a real tongue lashing, and many of the religious leaders over the years have made it their main emphasis to give a regular dose of criticism and fearful threatening to the believers in their care.

But the little boy was simply full of joy rather than any feeling of resentment or disappointment. his joy came from the fact that he had given of himself unconditionally without leaving out a single one!

If we look at the parable of the Prodigal Son, the son is like the thoughtless children. The second son is like the religious leaders – telling the father in the story how he SHOULD feel. But the father is like God. All he felt was joy! He had no room for any resentment or wrath or punishment. He did not say, "you can come back if you promise never to do that again!" "You can come back if you prove that you can live up to the following rules!" The father was simply full of joy because his son had finally come home!

I think that the God that I have come to know in my life is far more concerned with loving us than He is with judging us or condemning us! He is far more into the business of comforting us and helping us than He is of scaring us. He wants our love and trust, not our fear. He is full of joy because He has not missed a one of us! Not a single one!

* I found the basic story of the little boy on the Internet, from a person named Dale Galloway. The original source is unknown.

CHAPTER 33: DAISEY'S BOTTLE

There is a story that Paul Harvey told on his radio show, "The Rest of The Story". I can not attest to its accuracy, as his stories were, I think, on a few occasions more legend than history. But all of his stories were very interesting and this story is no exception. It is the story of Daisey's Bottle.

As the story goes, Daisey Alexander stood at the edge of the Thames River in London. It was in June of 1937. She threw a bottle into the river with a message inside. Where did it go? Did it wash ashore upriver? No. Perhaps it was dashed and broken on some rocks? No, again. According to those who know about tides and currents, it almost certainly had to have followed a course very similar to this:

After passing out of the river, it took a journey northward, past the Netherlands, Scotland, and Denmark. It went between the Shetland Island and the coast of Denmark into the vast North Atlantic Ocean. 1937 becomes 1938 and hundreds of miles of Norwegian coastline is left behind as the bottle floats through the Arctic Circle into the Barents Sea above the northern coast of the Soviet Union.

The currents have brought the bottle over Siberia. It has floated all during the long years of World War II. It has been almost ten years as it moves down into the Bering Strait between Siberia and Alaska, past the Aleutian Islands into the Northern Pacific. Finally it wonders down to the coast of Northern California, where it is half buried in the sand of a deserted San Francisco beach.

As the story continues, Jack Wurm, a 55 year old jobless man who is near penniless after the bankruptcy of his restaurant business, discovers the bottle. He sees a piece of paper inside and breaks it on a rock. He reads the following: "To avoid all confusion, I leave my entire estate to the lucky person who finds this bottle and to my attorney, Barry Cohen, share and share alike. Daisey Alexander, June 20, 1937.

 According to the story, it did stand up in court. It was the will and testament of an heir of the Singer Sewing Machine family, who had died in London in 1939. Jack Wurm of San Francisco inherited 6 million dollars from the bottle that had floated 12 thousand miles in almost 12 years at sea!

In a real sense, each of us is like that bottle. God threw each of us into the vast sea of life the day that we were born. The main difference between us and Daisey's bottle, is that the contents of the bottle blessed only two people, and that was only at the very end of the journey. But the contents of these vessels that we call Don and Bob and Jane and Fay – all of us, God sees to it that we bless thousands of souls beginning at the very moment that we are born. Think of the people you blessed when you were born – parents, family, doctor, nurses, friends. In school, growing up with friends, dating, school, marriage, family, work, retirement, church, interaction in the community – you were a vessel that contained unique talents and gifts that God placed there!

You are sensitive to God and your intention has been, whether you were fully aware of it or not, to bless the world. Such is the ingenious plan of God that even those folks who have no intention of blessing anyone, still even by their meanness and neglect and their negative influences, contribute to the blessing of others just as the wind and waves contributed to the journey of Daisey's bottle.

Each of you, with your sensitivity to God and your intention to bless others, make your daily contribution as you continue to "bob along" in God's great ocean called life. Your presence, your smile, your words of encouragement – all that you are - is a gift from God to His creation!

My Best To You Each Morning

CHAPTER 34: A HOLDING PATTERN

The incident that I am about to relate might be a bit confusing since you are likely not familiar with the locations that I am going to mention. So, if I seem to give too much detail it is simply my attempt to make the picture clear to you.

Our son, Dean, lives in Miami and comes home every Christmas to Augusta, Georgia (USA) – a distance of about 600 miles. In the past, it has been much more expensive to fly into Augusta than to some other cities like Atlanta or Savannah. So people have experimented with driving to Atlanta (about 125 miles from Augusta) or Savannah (about 120 miles) to begin or end their air journey. Most people who have tried doing that have given up the practice because it just was not practical. After the incident that I am going to relate, we gave it up too!

My son was flying on a quick, direct flight from Miami to Savannah. It would take him about two hours. Our drive to meet him in Savannah would take about the same amount of time. He was to arrive at 4:30 in Savannah and we would have a nice meal and return to Augusta. At 4:00 we were there with bells on. Shortly after we arrived at the airport it began to rain. It was not just a heavy rain, it was a "gulley washer"! By 4:30 the flight board was reading: "Flight 637 from Miami - delayed because of weather". At 5:00 it still said, "delayed". At 5:30 I went to talk with the nice lady at the desk to ask when she expected the flight to arrive.

She said, "Oh, it's here! It's up there in a 'holding pattern' because the weather here is too bad to attempt a landing!"

At 6:00 I asked again – still in a "holding pattern"! Dean finally landed at 7:00 – 2 and a half hours in a "holding pattern". During the holding pattern, the plane had run low on fuel and so it flew to Augusta to refuel and then flew back to Savannah. While the plane was in Augusta, Dean asked to be let off to take a taxi home, but the pilot refused.

Now, I told you about this incident to illustrate what I think is true of "Senior Citizens". When I think about the physical condition of so many of my friends – heart troubles, surgeries, many with disabilities, others recently passed – it occurs to me that we are all in a holding pattern of sorts. Someone said, in our Sunday School Department, that there is no place for our department to "promote to" except to our "final promotion"!

Yes, in a way we are all like the folks on Dean's flight from Miami. We too are in a "holding pattern". The difference is, those folks were anxious to be done with their holding pattern, whereas most of us want to continue in ours for as long as possible. We love our lives and we don't want the end to come – not yet anyway!

Perhaps that is why nature arranges for things to become more and more uncomfortable the longer our holding pattern continues. Our hearing diminishes, we develop pains here and there, and some of us lose some of our mental faculties. Our muscles get weaker and we just aren't the energetic young things we once were.

So, how should we think about that? We can be bitter. We can complain. We can even just quit everything and stay home. But I really think that there is a better way. Let me just mention several ideas that might serve us well as we contemplate our "holding pattern".

First of all, we need to remind ourselves that it is the nature of all things to be born, to mature, and then to die. You and I are a part of that nature! We should not expect to be exceptions to that rule!

Secondly, most of us have been blessed, already, with an abundance of life – both in the number of years and in the quality. If you read the obituary, as most of us do, you will notice that many folks do not enjoy near as many years as we have already enjoyed. I personally do not believe that those who die young are blessed any less than we are. Jesus was only 33 or so and I do not believe that he died "prematurely". I just think that God has his reasons for allowing some of us to walk a longer road than others. But, from our perspective at least, it is nice that we have had that opportunity.

Thirdly, we need to realize what the Apostle Paul realized. He said that "to be IN the body is to be absent from the Lord" (and the whole experience of whatever the hereafter has to offer) and that he was "willing to be

ABSENT from the body in order to be present with the Lord". (II Cor. 5). I think Paul was saying that whether we are HERE or THERE we are blessed either way - but being THERE is even a greater blessing.

Fourthly, While we are in this holding pattern we are not alone! We are all on the same "airplane". Whatever happens to one of us can happen to any of us, thus we should not be "smug"about our situation but compassionate and helpful to each other. As we continue to live, something WILL get sick, wear out, or quit so that we CAN go back to the Father. We are all in the same family. We love each other and we are all loved by the same Father.

Lastly, as each of us disembarks from our holding pattern, we do so with the confidence that we leave here only because our work is finished. We have other work ahead of us in another place. We leave with the love and respect of each other. We each will be valued and missed by the others – that is until we meet again!

Until that time we can each continue learning, serving God and each other, and enjoying life as long as God allows us to stay.

Then, as a poem once put it so beautifully about the boat that leaves people saying "good bye"on one shore only to be greeted by loved ones on another shore – when our holding pattern ends on this side we will be arriving to greetings from the folks waiting for us in Heaven.

CHAPTER 35: THE TIN CAN TELEPHONE

I am sure that many of you can remember the home-made toys that we had when we were children if you happen to be in that generation that grew up in the 1940's. We had stilts and rubber guns, and tin can telephones. Did you have a tin can telephone? All it took was two tin cans and a length of string!

To make the tin can telephone, you would take two cans, about the size that vegetables would come in, and make a small hole in the middle of the can bottom. Then you would put the end of a length of sting through the hole in one can and tie a knot so that the string would not come back out. Then you would tie the other end to the second can in a similar manner.

The length of string could be any length up to a city block long. Then, one kid would take one can and another kid would walk the other can to the full length of the string. Then the talker would talk into one can while the listener would put his ear to his can to hear. Then the can positions would be reversed and the listener would answer the first talker.

In my neighborhood we had an alley between each two streets. The back of the houses would face the alley. Many of the houses had second stories with porches on the back. We would have one kid on one second story porch with a telephone. Then, across the alley on another second story porch would be another phone, with a string connecting the two. The distance would probably be from 75 to 100 feet. That was our version of "texting".

When I thought of the tin can telephone recently, it occurred to me how much that telephone was like communicating with God in prayer.

There are three things that are very important with a tin can telephone. First, unlike modern telephones, you could only do one thing at a time - you could talk or you could listen. But you could not do both at the same time! Sometimes, when we pray, we wonder why we do not seem to hear God speaking to us. We might say, "I pray to God every day but I can't really say that I sense God's answer. The problem might be that, we are so intent on asking God to do something or telling God this or that, that God just can't get a word in at all.

The second thing about a tin can phone is, if the string touches a tree or telephone pole or anything else, the voice transmission over the string is broken and you won't hear anything but static. If we try to pray and we have anything at all between ourselves and God that acts as a source of interference, then we will not be able to converse with God. Only you can determine what that something might be, but it could be something as simple as "business".

Sometimes we get so busy with "things". It might be good things, even church things. Jesus was busy every day with "church things" - preaching, teaching, healing - but he still took time to get off by himself, away from everybody and everything, in order to talk with the Father. If we find that something is an interference with our prayer life, then we need to simply decide, "is this thing really more important than having a conversation with the Father?"

The third thing about a tin can phone is, you have to keep the line tight at all times. If the string sags, it will not transmit the message. I would equate the slack line on a tin can phone with a lack of sincerity on our part when we are trying to pray. If we are just praying because "it is time to pray" or because we think prayer is something that we ought to do, then we might not be very sincere.

To me, sincerity in prayer means being willing to say, "Dear God, here I am. I am willing to be anything, do anything, or go anywhere that you desire. Like the man in the Bible that said, "Lord I believe - help Thou my unbelief", we need to say, "Lord, I truly want to be sincere. Please help me where I am insincere."

God knows us better than we know ourselves. Sincerity is simply not trying to hide anything at all from God.

I saw an interesting commercial the other day - you might have seen it too. Someone in a restaurant was supposedly communicating with one of the cooks in the kitchen over a tin can telephone. But whoever produced the commercial obviously did not know anything about how a tin can telephone works. The string was not tight and it draped over all sorts of things before it reached the receiver can.

I thought to myself, "There is no way in the world that the supposed message is getting through on this commercial!" It is as futile as if someone were trying to yell a message to someone a thousand miles away. When we try to pray to God without sincerity or by doing all the talking or allowing interference, then it is just as much an exercise in futility.

May God bless us by helping us to pray more effectively and sincerely, reducing any interference that we may find between ourselves and Him.

CHAPTER 36: PLEASING GOD, IF'S AND BUT'S

Do you like Cajun jokes? Here is one: Boudreaux and Little Piere were sitting on the dock fishing and their conversation went something like this. Little Piere, he say, "Oh Boudreaux. You are so big and strong! I do declare. If I was as big and strong as you, you know what I would do?"

"No, what would you do, Little Piere?" said Boudreaux.

"Well," said Piere, "I been thinkin. You know all those alligators out there in the bayou, they skins bring lots of money from them tourists. If I was big and strong like you I would run down to that bayou and I would find the biggest, meanest alligator I could find and I would wrestle him and get his big old skin and sell it! That's what I would do if I was big and strong like you!"

"Well, I been thinkin too," said Boudreaux, "and I do believe that they's some other alligators out there in the bayou that's just about yo size!"

There is an old saying that goes like this: "If our 'ifs' and 'buts' were candy and nuts, then we'd all have a Merry Christmas". Let me say that again. "If our 'ifs' and 'buts' were candy and nuts, then we'd all have a Merry Christmas".

Little Piere thought, "if only I was big and strong!" BUT, his awareness of his limitations kept him from seeing the possibilities!

Do you ever find yourself thinking like this - "If only I had a stronger faith...but my faith is so weak!" Or "I wish that I could do something really important for God, but about all I do for God is go to church!" Or, "If I had more talent and could teach a Sunday School class..or sing in the choir...". Or "If only I were young again I could be a missionary, BUT that time has come and gone!"

If you have been doing any of that "If only...BUT I can't" thinking lately, then I would like to say that the Bible is sprinkled with stories and teachings that might just give you a new vision of the possibilities. Let's think for a moment about those thoughts that I just mentioned.

First, "If only I had a stronger faith, but..." I often get bogged down with this. I find myself wishing that God would work a miracle with me like He did with Paul, so that I would never have another doubt about my faith. But then I remember how very low Jesus set the bar where faith is concerned. He never said, " To please the Father you've got to have a really strong faith!" No. All he said was, "If you can have even a little bit of faith, even as much as a mustard seed, then you can do everything that God wants you to do!"

The second thought was this: "I wish I could do something important for God". There is a story in Acts which tells of the conversion of Saul. Saul was made temporarily blind when he experienced Jesus on the road to Damascus. He was taken to the home of Judas in Damascus. God asked a man named Ananias to go visit

Saul at Judas' home. Ananias was afraid to go at first but
he finally did go and as a result Saul regained his sight.
No doubt Ananias had often wished that he could do
something important for God. But it turned out that all
God needed him to do was make a visit. But it was truly
an important visit.

Perhaps you have been saying, if only I could do
something really important for God BUT I am too old,
too limited, etc". But perhaps all that God really needs
you to do is send a card, make a phone call, visit a shut
in or someone in a Nursing Home, or perhaps give some
encouragement to one of our Ministers. Yet, that might
be just as important today as Ananias' visit was in Paul's
day.

The third thought was this: "If I just had more talent I
could teach a Sunday School class...or sing in the
choir...BUT I can't." I think about the story of Mary and
Martha and Jesus. You remember that Jesus came to
visit the sisters and Mary immediately sat at his feet and
listened. Martha, instead, started the great smells in the
kitchen that began to make Jesus hungry. Soon , Martha
said, "Jesus, I am in here fixing lunch and Mary is just
sitting there. Would you please make her come in and
help me?"

But Jesus said, in effect, "You have chosen to do an
important thing and I can hardly wait to taste your
wonderful lunch. But Mary has chosen to listen to my
teaching and that is important too. I don't want to take
that away from her." That is the way we usually leave

the story, with Martha seeming to be obsessing over trivialities. But I do believe, if the situation had been reversed, that Jesus would have applied the same rule. If Mary had said, "Jesus, Martha really needs to hear this, please make her stop rattling those pots and pans and come in here with us!" I truly believe that Jesus would have said, "Mary, Martha has chosen to honor me with what she does best and what she is doing is important too and I don't want to take that away from her"

I think that this story was recorded so that we all might realize that God has made us each different with different talents and interests and inclinations, and that He honors and appreciates how each of us chooses to serve Him. I think the principle here is: "Whatever you feel lead to do for God is blessed and appreciated by Him. I think that the Father knows our strengths and limitations and, rather than comparing us with others, He accepts whatever we do for Him as very important, whether we are the teacher or the listener - the singer or the one who appreciates the song.

Lastly, "If I were young again I might have been a missionary or a full time Christian worker, BUT I am not young anymore!" There is a story in the Old Testament that, I think, speaks to that. Early in David's career, while he and his followers were away from home, The Amalekites raided his village, burned everything, and took the wives and cattle of David and his men. David went after the enemy with 600 men. But 200 of the men became tired and could go no further. David let them stay with the extra equipment while the other 400 went with David. They conquered the enemy and brought back not only their own families and possessions, but also many other things which we call the spoils of war.

Some of the 400 men who "did all the work", wanted to say that the 200 men who minded the stuff could not have a portion of the spoils that they brought back. But David made it a law that day that those who stay behind to "mind the stuff" would always be considered part of the team and would deserve credit the same as those who actually carried out the project.

I believe that God still honors that principle today. If you ever find yourself saying, "If only I could be a Missionary, Preacher, Church Leader, a special worker for God", please remember this: If you pray for those folks, if you encourage them or support them in any way, you are "minding the stuff" and God is smiling on you.

A neighbor of ours, Dot Ashe, is not able to drive right now, so we did her grocery shopping for her last Wednesday. This neighbor, who has to use a walker any time she walks, even in her home, gave us her shopping list and it included peanut butter, Coolwhip, and four graham cracker crusts. We were curious and asked about these items. It turns out that she was making four pies - two for a nearby fire station and two for the police station at Daniel Village. If she were able to be a fireman or a policeman, I do not believe that she would be doing any more in the sight of God than she is doing as she "minds the stuff" for those who actually wear the uniforms.

I think the same is true as you and I encourage the church staff, bring food and clothes for benevolence, the Bridge Ministry, and the Burn Unit, or share our offerings for God's work around the world. Or, as our neighbor is doing, if you bake a pie for people who serve our community or for folks who have had a death in the family, you are minding the stuff for someone who needs it. If you ask God, He will even give you new ideas for doing that, just as He did for our neighbor.

If our 'If' and 'buts' do become candy and nuts and other good things, then lots of folks will have a merrier Christmas and a happier life!

CHAPTER 37: Row, Row, Row Your Boat

All of us have sung this song as a round in our younger days. It was fun! But did you ever think that it actually has some very good advice for everyday living? In fact, it gives the basis for a rather sound philosophy of life! I would like to show you what I mean by taking each line and giving you my own interpretation of its advice.

Row your BOAT! There is a sense in which everyone that is born is in the SAME boat. We all live on the same small planet in community. What one of us does effects all of the others. But, in another sense, each of us is born alone and we die alone. We add other individuals to our lives and we sometimes come to believe that they are essentially part of us, but they are not. I personally believe that each of us is an eternal personality and that we are issued a "temporary" boat or body/mind in which to travel during our temporary stay on earth. So, each of us is in our little "boat", traveling down the stream of life together.

ROW your boat! This indicates that the purposeful movement of our boat takes some effort on our part. We do not just flip a switch, start a motor, and put our boat on autopilot! Perhaps, in a sense, our boat has never been launched. It is still on dry land. Because of family environment, fear, or some other reason, we are really not living our own lives yet! Or, perhaps we are being towed by someone else, with no sense of having control over our own lives or being our "own person". At any rate, the admonition to "row" means that I must willfully put my own hand to the oar and with some purposeful and consistent effort bring about some movement.

Row YOUR boat! Some of us might think that our primary job is to tend to someone else's boat – that of our children, our spouse, our friends. But it can not be done, and we should not even try. Kalil Gibran had it right when he said that our children are like arrows that we send from our bow. Once they are sent out, we have little ultimate control over their destiny. We can influence them (and our spouse, friends, etc.) but we are not supposed to be rowing THEIR boat. Have you ever played a game like basketball with a person next to you who tries to play not only their position but yours also? It is not only annoying but it keeps you from fully enjoying the game. That is exactly what happens when you try to row someone else's boat! And we should be just as careful not to let other people attempt to row OUR boat.

Row your boat, gently down the STREAM! Life is somewhat like a stream or river that we are all IN. We are in the stream whether we like it or not. The only way NOT to be in the stream is to withdraw from life – either in the sense of being a recluse or in the more drastic sense of ending our own life. This choice is made by some, but most of us stay in the river one way or another. We do have some choices. We can take our rowing very seriously and stay at it obsessively. We can get out on the bank and rest a while. We can have fun with the other rowers. There are probably as many choices as there are rowers. But we should try not to be too judgemental about how others choose to travel on the stream, as long as they do not hurt the other rowers.

Row gently DOWN the stream. So much of life is more difficult than it needs to be, because we try to do it without consulting our source – God. God made us with certain talents, inclinations, built – in goals, and purposes. If we seek to find what God intends for our life, then life becomes easier, like going down stream. When we try to fight what God intends us to be, it is like rowing constantly against the currents of life!

Row GENTLY down the stream. What is your typical approach to life? Do you approach each day feverishly, anxiously, fearfully, greedily? How? To approach life gently is to know that nothing else works as well. It is like the gardener who knows that, trying to make his plants grow faster by tugging on them just does not work well! Forcing things in life does not work as well as "gently". To approach life gently is to know that nothing else works as safely either – a gentle approach to animals, people, and situations keeps hurts at a minimum – theirs and yours. I have a 15 year old puppy dog, and when she looks at me with her gentle eyes, I know that "gently"is the best way to live life!

MERRILY, MERRILY, MERRILY! If "gently"is the way to APPROACH life, "merrily"is the way that we should FEEL about life. I am not saying that we should be like Pollyanna and not recognize that life has its difficulties. But I do believe that we create much of what we meet in life by the way that we FEEL about life. If we approach life every day with a feeling of fear, suspicion, expecting the worse, depression, boredom, lacking purpose, then these feelings will color everything that you experience. I know that we can not always control our feelings, but, to the extent that we can, MERRILY beats every negative feeling "hands down"!

Life is but a DREAM! I must confess that I am not sure what the author of this song had in mind at this point, but I will give you my thoughts for what they are worth. If you think for a moment of the possibility (some of us would say the probability) that there is an eternal "hereafter" that all of us will eventually participate in, then the eternal existence of each of us is more primary than this temporary life span that we are now experiencing.

So, as our day time, conscious existence is longer and more primary than our brief night time dream states, then our life time on earth is just a brief "dream"compared to our eternal life. I am not saying that our life on earth is not important. It is VERY important, just as our dream time every night is important. Scientists say that our dream state is a time in which our whole body/mind is greatly benefited. In the same sense, the "dream"that we are living on earth is a time in which our whole spiritual growth is benefited. But, just as we do not take too seriously any monsters or disasters that we encounter in our dreams, so we should not take the disasters and misfortunes that we encounter in this earth life too seriously.

So, next time you find yourself taking life too seriously or feeling the stress of your work, your family, or even your spiritual life, take a few minutes to remember the words of that cute little song:

ROW, ROW, ROW, YOUR BOAT

GENTLY DOWN THE STREAM,

MERRILY, MERRILY, MERRILY, MERRILY,

LIFE IS BUT A DREAM!

My Best To You Each Morning

CHAPTER 38: GIVING PERMISSION

There is a story, related by Paul Harvey*, about a boy named Joey. As a child, his mother had high hopes of him becoming a fine violinist and started him very early on violin lessons. Each week she would give him money for the lesson and he would go after school. This he did for years. Many of the children teased him and called him "sissy".

When he got older, one of his friends became an amateur boxer and invited Joey to go with him to the gym. He talked Joey into sparring with him. Joey knocked him down and almost out! The friend said, "Joey, forget about the violin! You're a born boxer!" After that Joey would go to the gym instead of his violin lessons. He didn't feel right about using his violin money to pay for gym, but he was afraid to tell his mother.

When he began to get boxing matches, he was afraid that his mother would see his name in the newspaper, so he used his middle name instead of his last name. And so Joey became Joe Louis, the Brown Bomber! He was the heavyweight boxing champion of the world during my childhood years of the 1940's.

Now, a very important part of this story is that someone recognized Joey's true talent and encouraged him, gave him "permission" to believe in himself and to have hope of becoming what he dreamed of. Joey might have gone on to play the violin as an amateur. He might even have become a professional. And that would have been O.K. But he had the ability to become the heavyweight champion of the world. Still, he needed someone to "give him permission to dream"!

It might be a good idea for each of us to ask God to make us sensitive to the talents that He has placed in the people that we make contact with every day.

When I was in the fourth grade, I heard a person play a live concert with the violin. It was the first time I had heard anything like that! It brought tears to my eyes. It made me want to play an instrument myself. I mentioned it to my adult cousin and she said, "Maybe you can do that some day!" That is all she said. But it made it O.K. for me to hope for that! When I got to the seventh grade I began to learn to play the tuba. When I was in the ninth grade I switched to trombone. My cousin's brief affirmation helped open up a life time of musical interest to me.

You might have a friend who has always wanted to paint, but thinks, "I am too old to start now!" Perhaps if you said, "You are NEVER too old if you really want to do it!", it might make all the difference in the world to him.

When I was 13 years old I had a cousin who lived near me in Savannah, Georgia. He was about ten and "looked up to me". I used to draw him pictures of airplanes. I gave him a book that my father, a sign painter, had given to me about the basics of how to draw. Shortly after that I moved away and I did not see him again until I was about 50 years old. I was in downtown Augusta and noticed a graphics studio. Since the name was "Ellis Graphics", (his last name), I was curious enough to go in and check. My cousin, whom I had not seen in all of those years, had made a career of drawing. I do not claim total credit for that, of course. But I think I had a part in it!

So, if you ask God to give you the ministry of affirmation and a sensitivity to the potentials in the lives of your friends, children, grand children, children in your church and neighborhood, there is no telling how many new talents He might send your way for you to help discover!

What talents do YOU have? Do you crochet or knit? Do you embroider? Men, do you work with wood? Finetta, my wife, learned to embroider from her mother and she learned crochet and knitting from older women after she was grown. She has since passed these skills on to others.

I learned to use a hand saw and a coping saw from my father when I was six years old. Later, after I was married, I saw a friend making a dulcimer (a stringed musical instrument), He made dulcimers as a career. He charged $50.00 at that time, and I could not afford that. He said, "Here is some wood and a pattern. Make one yourself!" I applied what I had learned when I was six years old and, with a coping saw, I made a dulcimer. I went on to make over 200 dulcimers and other instruments over the next several years. But my friend had given me "permission".

You never know when some little something that you know might "take root" in another person.So, why not do this: Ask God to help you be mindful of interests or talents expressed by other people.Then be willing to affirm that person. Encourage him or her to follow the talent or interest if that is his wish.Your permission to hope or try something might make all the difference in that person developing a hobby, a talent, or even a career.

When I was in the tenth grade I had been feeling that God was calling me into the ministry. But I was afraid to mention it, even to my parents. But a math teacher, Mrs. Virgie Cone, asked me one day what I was interested in as a career. I told her what I was feeling. Her sensitivity to this sixteen year old boy gave me permission to think that, maybe I could be a minister. This lead to a minstry that spanned thirty five years and still goes on.

So, maybe there are some young people within your scope of influence. Maybe there is an adult who would be willing to try something new if you are willing to give him or her just a word of encouragement or a simple first lesson in some skill or hobby that you already know something about.

Try an experiment with me. Some day when you have some time, take a piece of paper and make a list of any children or young people that you have contact with - in your church, your neighborhood, or your own family. Ask God to give you an opportunity to talk with one of these about his hobbies, his hopes for a career, or talents that he/she would like to develop. Give him encouragement, information, and respect for his ability. Give him permission to hope. Perhaps this might open up a whole new ministry in your own life.

That teacher, who asked me what I wanted to do with my life back when I was sixteen, had her 99th birthday three years ago. My wife and I went to her party, over a hundred miles away. Sixty years had passed but I had not forgotten what she meant to my life. God might give you the gift of having that meaning in another person's life - maybe a young person - maybe a "not so young" person.

* More of Paul Harvey's The Rest Of The Story, by Paul Aurandt

CHAPTER 39: MY THANKSGIVING HOLIDAY

My extended family planned to meet for Thanksgiving at our retreat spot, the Hermitage, on Oval lake. I was concerned because one of the highlights of the retreat each year is the "Devotional", a short message delivered just prior to our big meal.

This was my year to "devote" and my complete absence of ideas seemed to me a harbinger of my being a source of shame to my family.

One evening, as I was searching for a theme, I noticed that "Fiddler on the Roof" was on the evening movie list.

The movie is about Tevye, the village milk man, and his wife and daughters. The setting is Tsarist Russia in 1905. Tevye and his wife, Golde, were married in the traditional Jewish way, chosen for each other by a "match maker", with no thought of love or personal choice on the part of either.

Their lives were complicated because their three older daughters, within a short time, had made choices of husbands that defied their beloved tradition. The first daughter, after being promised to the local, well- to- do butcher, persuaded Tevye to give his permission for her to marry a poor tailor instead. Tevye did this, in spite of tradition, because he saw the "love in her eyes" for the tailor.

This new experience of seeing love and marriage together caused Tevye to rethink his own marriage, and as he approached Golde a very beautiful song ensued.

Tevye: "Do you love me?"

Golde: "Do I what!?"

Tevye: "Do you love me?"

Golde: "Do I love you? For 25 years I've washed your clothes, cooked your meals, given you children. After 25 years, why talk about love right now?"

Tevye: The first time I met you was on our wedding day. I was scared."

Golde: "I was shy."

Tevye: "But my father and my mother said we'd learn to love each other, and now I am asking. Golde, do you love me?"

Golde: "I'm your wife!"

Tevye: "I know, but do you love me?"

Golde: "Do I love him? For 25 years I've lived with him, fought with him, starved with him. If that is not love, what is?"

Tevye: "Then you love me."

Golde: "I suppose I do."

Tevye: "And I suppose I love you too."

Both: "It doesn't change a thing. But even so, after 25 years it's nice to know."

Now, as I heard this tender interchange, it dawned on me that this could be a conversation between God and myself. Let me present it to you just as I heard it.

God: "Donald, do you love me?"

Myself: "Do I what?"

God: "Do you love me?"

Myself: "Do I love you? I must be imagining this!"

God: "Donald. This is God and I am asking you a question. Do you love me?"

Myself: "God, I'm a Christian!"

God: "I know, but do you love me?"

Myself: "Do I love Him? For over 60 years I have prayed to Him, talked to other people about Him, even built my career on Him. If that is not love, what is?"

God: "Then you do love me?"

Myself: "God, if I know my heart, I do love you!"

God: "And, I love you too! It really does not change a thing, but even so - After 60 years it's nice to know!"

The season of Thanksgiving and Christmas seem to me to be a time when God is again singing to each of us, "Do you love me?" And each of us, in our own way, must look into our heart and answer as we see fit. For God might keep asking until we answer.

Prayer: Dear Father. We DO love You. Help us to love You more. Amen.

CHAPTER 40: LITTLE THINGS MEAN A LOT

 I am indebted to my friend, Jean Kearns, and her blog for reintroducing me to a song of the 50's. As soon as I saw it on her Encouragement Blog, I knew that it would appear, sooner or later, in a devotional. It is not a Christmas song as such, but I would like to share it with you now during this Christmas season. So, here goes. See if you remember:

"Blow me a kiss from across the room, say I look nice when I'm not

Touch my hair when you pass my chair, little things mean a lot.

Give me your arm as you cross the street, call me at six on the dot,

A line a day when you're far away, little things mean a lot.

You don't have to buy me diamonds and pearls, champagne, sables and such. I never cared much for diamonds and pearls, cause honestly, Honey, they just cost money.

Give me a hand when I've lost my way, give me a shoulder to cry on,

Whether the day is cloudy or bright, give me your heart to rely on.

Send me the warmth of your secret smile, to show me you haven't forgot,

For now and forever, that's always and ever,

Little things mean a lot."

That song says so much. There are wives who have everything that money can buy, except the little words and touches that can make them really happy. Many a child has all of the expensive presents when all he really wants are words like, "I'm proud of you, son!"

When we come to Christmas time, it isn't really the expensive presents you remember, it is a tree ornament you got as a child, or the one your own child picked out just for you. Your precious Christmas memories might include the time when your son, in his own hand writing, wrote, "Merry Christmas, Mommie. I love you." or you lifted your little girl up so she could put the star "on the very tippy top" of the Christmas tree. It is the little things that mean so much at Christmas time. Perhaps it is a note that you got on some Christmas past that you keep in a special box somewhere close to your heart. It is the little things that mean a lot!

Maybe there are some "little things" we can do this Christmas to add joy to someone's life. Perhap, as part of our Christmas preparation, we could make a list of some little things we might do to add to someone's Christmas joy. Do you remember when your child sang her ABC's to you, ending with "Now I've said my ABC's, tell me what you think of me!"? Why not send a note this Christmas and tell someone "what you think of them"?

Perhaps send a few Christmas cards to folks who are not on your list. A phone call, email, or a visit might be just the little thing that someone needs to give them some encouragement. Why not make a list and try it this Christmas? Little things mean a lot.

Well, as I was making a list of things to get this Christmas for my family, I found myself asking not only what each of them might enjoy but also what they probably would not enjoy.

Then I thought, "If God was on my Christmas list, what would I get Him. What would He enjoy getting from me? What would He NOT want?"

I thought of I Corinthians 13, in which Paul says that God wants us to have love in our hearts. He says that even if we could speak the words of men and Angels but did not have love behind those words, it would sound like a noisy gong to God. So God wants us to have love in our hearts. But this gives me a problem. Only God can create love in my heart. I can't turn real love on and off! I can't WILL myself to be motivated by love!

So, that brings up the second thing that God wants from us. He wants love but he also wants fellowship with His childrem! If I can not create love in my heart like God wants from me, I must turn to God and ask Him, like David did when he said,"create in me a clean heart, Oh God." I must say, "God, please create love in my heart. I can't do it by myself!" They say that dependence on God is the key to intimacy with God. That is how you have fellowship with God. You must feel your need of Him.

When you have fellowship with God you develop gratitude, which is the third thing that God wants from us. Gratitude is like a magic wand that can change our whole outlook on life in a matter of minutes. Gratitude is a key to happiness! Gratitude can change any of the negative conditions known to man into joy and happiness in a very short time. Our illness, depression, fear, hatred, regret, and all other awful burdens can be melted away in minutes by a heart felt gratitude. Gratitude comes from fellowship with God.

So God wants three little things, that mean a lot to Him - Love, Fellowship, and Gratitude. He doesn't want these three things because He needs them for himself. He wants them because He knows that they are three Keys to our own happiness.

We can give God our fellowship wrapped in such thoughts as these: "God, please help me with this problem, I really need you!" We can show our gratitude when we say something like, "I really had a good time at the movie tonight, Lord. Thank you for bringing that into my life!" And we can send love with something as simple as, "Good morning, God! I just wanted to say, "I love you!". We don't even have to use words. We can just look up to God like my puppy dog does when his look says, "I am depending on you for whatever comes next in my life because you are the boss!" Or it can be like my wife's smile when it says, " I really, really love you - more than words can say!" God loves to hear our words, our thoughts, even our looks!

So, this Christmas, little things mean a lot to God as it does to each of us. I think that if He put His words into a song it might sound something like this: (To tune of "Little Things Mean a Lot").

"Laugh with me when you're feeling good, cry with me when you're not,

Share with Me any problems you have, Little things mean a lot.

Think of Me when you see a rainbow, remember I haven't forgot,

Be a friend to the neighbor who needs you, Little things mean a lot.

You don't have to give me long winded prayers, especially when not from your heart,

I've never cared much for long winded prayers, they may sound nice but they make me weary -

Help someone else as I've done for you, help them to know that I love them,

Share the forgiveness I've given to you, let it refresh and renew them.

Give me a smile when your day is done, Whether a good day or not,

I'm with you forever, good, bad, or whatever,

Little things mean a lot."

Prayer: Dear Father, may each person who hears the words of this song in our heart, remember that, to God, to our friends, to our family and even to the person on the street that we do not even know - Little things of love mean a lot! Amen

THE END